Battleground E

The Battle of
AUBERS RIDGE

With the continued expansion of the Battleground series a **Battleground Series Club** has been formed to benefit the reader. The purpose of the Club is to keep members informed of new titles and to offer many other reader-benefits. Membership is free and by registering an interest you can help us predict print runs and thus assist us in maintaining the quality and prices at their present levels.

Please call the office 01226 734555, or send your name and address along with a request for more information to:
Battleground Series Club Pen & Sword Books Ltd,
47 Church Street, Barnsley, South Yorkshire S70 2AS

Battleground Europe

The Battle of
AUBERS RIDGE

EDWARD HANCOCK

Series editor
Nigel Cave

Pen & Sword
MILITARY

First published in 2005 by
LEO COOPER
an imprint of
Pen & Sword Books Limited
47 Church Street, Barnsley, South Yorkshire S70 2AS

Copyright © Edward Hancock 2005

ISBN 1 84415 093 3

A CIP catalogue of this book is available
from the British Library

Printed by Redwood Books Limited
Trowbridge, Wiltshire

*For up-to-date information on other titles produced under the Leo Cooper imprint,
please telephone or write to:*
Pen & Sword Books Ltd, FREEPOST, 47 Church Street
Barnsley, South Yorkshire S70 2AS
Telephone 01226 734222

CONTENTS

Indian infantry carrying Maxims into action.

Introduction by Series Editor

Aubers Ridge is one of the set-piece battles that the small British Expeditionary Force initiated in the late winter and spring of 1915: Neuve Chapelle in March, Aubers in early May and itself almost immediately followed by Festubert. To the north the BEF had had the fight of its life at Second Ypres, a battle made all the more awful by the introduction, for the first time against the British and French, of poisonous gas. These were hard fighting months for the still very small force of British troops on the Continent, though by historical standards by then it was the biggest expeditionary force the British had ever sent abroad. But if they were hard fighting months for the BEF, they were extremely hard for the French. 1914 was the worst year of the war for the French army in terms of casualties, followed by 1915. 1916, the year of Verdun and the Somme, resulted in fewer casualties than both these years and 1918.

The relevance of these comments on casualties is to offer an explanation as to why the British offered battle when it was transparently obvious that it was ill-equipped so to do. Certainly, Neuve Chapelle had had some success and it had had the desired effect of forcing the Germans to reinforce their troop numbers opposite the British line. But it was an offensive desperately short of guns, which was to continue to be the refrain for the next eighteen months or so – really only in the very final stages of the Battle of the Somme could the BEF be said to have been reasonably well equipped with heavy artillery and suitable shells. Yet the attacks went ahead, in locations which tactically no British commander favoured.

The reason has to lie in the nature of allied warfare, with Britain very much the junior partner, with France carrying the major burden and the British being seen to co-operate and do their bit. Given the size of French casualties, a decision to halt an attack after a setback would not have been regarded in an understanding manner by the French staff – or popular opinion. Strictly military considerations rarely were the deciding factor in offensives of the Great War. Aubrs Ridge has to be seen bearing these considerations in mind if there is to be any hope of understanding what transpired to be the sheer futility of it all.

Nigel Cave
Ely Place, London

INTRODUCTION

During the winter of 1914-1915 the Central Powers (Germany and Allies) had continually fought against the Russian army on the eastern front without conclusive advance. East Prussia had been re-occupied and the Austro – Hungarian army had some success in the Carpathians, but the Russian front remained intact and no strategic gains, so vital to successful conquest, had been accomplished. The German Supreme Command planned a major offensive on the Russian front during the spring of 1915. To achieve the planned fighting strength an additional 100,000 men with a full complement of heavy artillery were drafted, mainly by using units from the western front, to form the Eleventh

The Allied Offensives 1915.

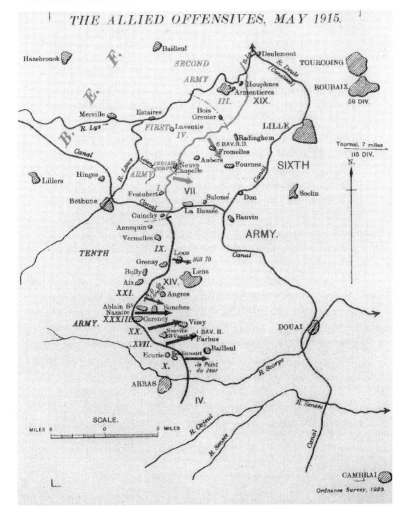

THE ALLIED OFFENSIVES, MAY 1915.

Ordnance Survey, 1928.

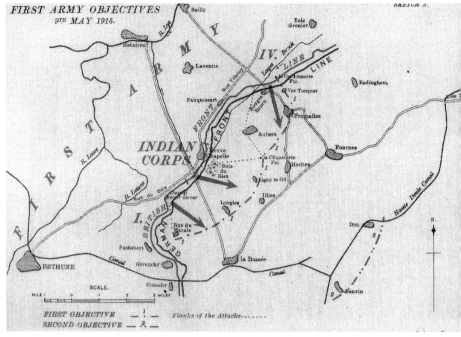

First Army Objectives 9 May 1915.

Army. This redeployment exposed to the Allied Powers an opportunity to break the German hold on the western front, recover lost ground and to inflict a crippling blow against the forces of the Central Powers before success in the east could enable the full might of the German army to be employed against them.

The crease in the flat landscape of northern France known as Aubers Ridge is situated a short distance south west of Lille, the city which in 1914, after its capture and occupation by the German army, became established as a centre of major military importance, and continued as a command, communication, and supply centre throughout the Great War, for their armies in the northern sector of the western front.

The country around Aubers, situated some thirty kilometres due south of the city of Ypres (Ieper) along the opposing trench lines, is well worth investigation on the well travelled journey between Ypres and the Somme, and is indeed itself an intriguing area which warrants a separate visit should time permit. It is situated ten kilometres south of Armentières, the British garrison town whose ladies were praised and forever immortalised in song, a further twenty kilometres south lies the important industrial town of Lens and the scene of the Loos battle, then a further ten kilometres, Vimy Ridge and Arras.

Living in Northern France during the 1990s allowed me the

8

opportunity to foster first hand my interest in the Western Front conflict. My knowledge was, as with many, initially confined to the well-documented battles that took place around Ypres and on the Somme. Travelling around the area my knowledge rapidly expanded to include the clashes that had continued day and night elsewhere between the opposing forces and I began to appreciate more the dilemmas faced by their commanders. I never cease to wonder at the very existence of the private soldier through those war years in primitive trench conditions, sun, rain, snow and ice, but invariably wet and muddy, summer and winter.

Writing in the 1930's Private Frank Richards D C M, M M recalled the primitive conditions in this sector in early 1915, cold and plagued by never ending water and mud. Hard frosty weather was preferred – easier to move about and to keep warm – and shirts could be hung out at night in an attempt to freeze out 'the crawlers'. He remembers there being plentiful supplies of sandbags, barbed wire, duckboards and other trench materials, and that a regular ration of coke could be collected from rear stores – across a 'corduroy' track snaking back across the ground, there being no communication trench. Sufficient jam, bully beef and biscuits were available – many duckboards were broken up and used for warming food and water for tea on braziers improvised by holing buckets scrounged from the now empty village nearby. Water, for drinking and cooking, was drawn from a willow ditch which ran across No Man's Land, although strictly forbidden. Even the discovery of decomposing bodies in close proximity did not stop the practice – he states 'our insides

Lieutenant R C Money works a hand pump in a communication trench after rain – near Bois Grenier.

Corduroy track snaking across marshy lands.

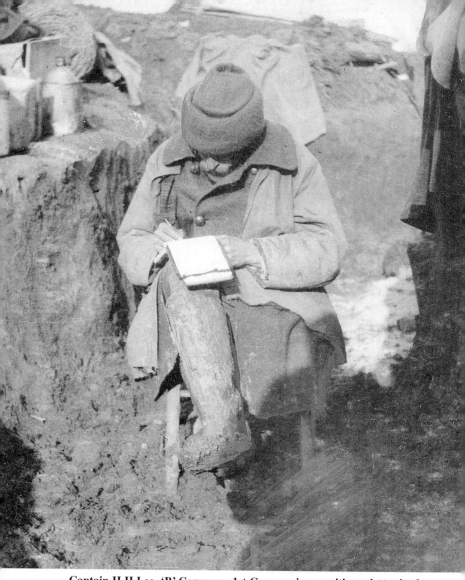

Captain H H Lee, 'B' Company, 1st Cameronians, writing a letter in the trenches. Grande Flamengrie Farm (Bois Grenier Sector), 11th February 1915.

were now as tough as the outsides of our bodies'. Trench periscopes were issued about this time, reducing the danger from snipers' bullets – but not before a fellow soldier of 2/Welsh Fusiliers, Private PJ Stevens, was struck in the head and killed as they stood side by side. Private Stevens is buried in Bois Grenier Communal Cemetery.

By visits to the cemeteries maintained by the Commonwealth War

Graves Commission I became aware of the soldiers of many nations who perished and lie buried hereabouts, either in the cemeteries or still remaining on the fields of battle. Canadians, New Zealanders, Australians, South Africans and from many other parts of the Empire, of the Indian Army, Moslem, Hindu, Gurkha and Sikh, and Chinese, Portuguese and of course many thousands of Frenchmen, suffered and died with the German invaders, as they fought to resist and repel.

The scenarios of the particular battles at Neuve Chapelle, Aubers Ridge and Festubert became clearer as my knowledge of the area, and of the situations of the adversaries, increased. Resistance to the westward advance of the German army had, by the winter of 1914, resulted, with a late flurry of attacks, counter attacks and strategic repositioning, in a line of opposing trenches being established, the higher, dryer, defensible length of Aubers Ridge being in German occupation.

This period of the war seems particularly to expose the horrors caused by the disparity between the strategic objectives of the ruling military minds

Periscopes avoided the attention of snipers.

and, against a background of production inadequacy and unsophisticated methods of communication, the blunt techniques open to achieve them. The patriotic enthusiasms which fuelled incredible sacrifices, which in turn wrought sudden and far reaching social shocks and changes, were manifest in the thousands of men repeatedly charging across the flat land into streams of murderous fire and explosions. The scenes are very easy to imagine in this quiet rural area studded with farms and villages which, although in parts much rebuilt, has altered little in general topography since the days of the conflict.

This part of France is easily reached, delightful to visit and rich in history; the choice of food and wine is wide and invariably very good, and the local French people I have always found to be most helpful, friendly and welcoming.

After considering various ways of describing the action of 9th May 1915 I concluded the least confusing and most satisfactory was to report separately the movement and involvement of each battalion. This method of presentation does tend to break up the continuity of the action. Please bear in mind when reading through this account of the battle, that at zero hour the men of all the leading platoons on both fronts all rose as one to attack across No Man's Land.

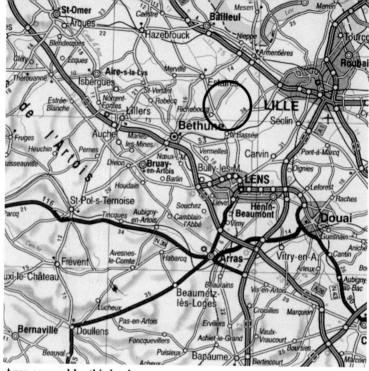

Area covered by this book.

LIST OF MAPS

ACKNOWLEDGEMENTS.

Individual acknowledgement of the large number of people who have assisted me in compiling this guidebook is regrettably not possible, suffice to say that each piece of information I have been given, however small and from whatever source, is greatly appreciated, and to each contributor I register my sincere thanks.

As always, thanks above all to the countless soldier scribes of all ranks and nationalities who jotted and wrote and recorded their experiences and thoughts and described what they saw around them in letters, diaries, and documents, official and personal; and to those who saved and preserved these items. Thanks also to the many authors who have since written accounts of the encompassing events and others who have compiled the available wealth of technical information concerning all the paraphernalia of the Great War.

My thanks to the many friendly members of staff of Records Offices, Newspaper Offices and Regimental Museums who, with cheerful mien, have invariably helped beyond the call of duty and often at short notice. Thanks also to members of the historical group of Laventie, and in particular to M. Octave Defief. Now retired, M. Defief farmed land adjoining the Rue Bacquerot for many years and provided me with much unsolicited detail of the surrounding area and local information. His father tilled the land before him and served in the French Army on the Somme front whilst his then enemy took possession of the farm, first in October 1914, and again in 1918. The experience was repeated during the Second World War. His son has for many years been tilling the same land under EEC policies now thankfully agreed around a table and common to us all.

I record my great appreciation for the assistance, encouragement and sympathy, of local people, manifest on several occasions. When fuel tanks ran unexpectedly dry in a most inhospitable situation; when the car became bogged down off road and somewhat isolated; being welcomed in for coffee breaks after lingering alone and forlorn with camera whilst persistent mist and gloom threatened to spoil photographic expeditions; being lifted by a smiling farmer with tractor after slipping and sliding across fields, dripping wet and mud bespattered, whilst rain sheeted down and time was rapidly running out; and when travellers, hungry, thirsty, and bedraggled, arrived out of hours speaking deutsche – franglais to be graciously served a most delicious and welcome meal. To the French people, whose *joie de vivre* has lightened such moments and who, with Gallic shrugs, have reminded us that sunshine is not far away, profound thanks.

Again I thank the staffs of the National Record Office, for so long familiar as the PRO, the Imperial War Museum, the Commonwealth War Graves Commission, the Volksbund Deutsche Kreigsgraberfursorge, the Deutsche Bundesarchiv and the National Army Museum, as well as members of the Western Front Association and other friends. All have provided over many months, information and assistance, maps, records and photographs, invaluably contributing to my understanding and the untangling of the events of the subject day. My gratitude to all at Pen and Sword Military Books, and in particular to Paul and Roni Wilkinson, who with good humour and patience have suffered my delays and alterations, and last, but by no means least, again my thanks to the editor of the Battleground Europe Series, Nigel Cave, for his constructive and helpful criticisms, and enduring patience in correcting copy and moulding my occasional flights of poetic fancy into more or less acceptable English.

I alone am responsible for any inaccuracies or omissions and hope that any unwitting errors will be forgiven.

ADVICE TO TOURERS

The access routes to suggested start points of the tour of the battlefield are detailed at the beginning of Chapter 8. The IGN Carte Vert series map (1/100000) No 2 Lille – Dunkerque shows the road network over the whole area, whilst the IGN Carte Bleu maps (1/25000) are ideal for local navigation. Map reference nos. 2404E (Lens) and 2405E (Armentières) cover the immediate subject areas of this book. These are available in the UK from Elstead Maps Ltd, Elstead, Surrey, GU 8 6JE Tel 01252 703472 or, for members, through the Western Front Association, who are also able to supply the relevant trench maps. In France local *Libraire* or *Maison de Presse* normally carry stocks of the IGN series. The towns nearest to the battlefield area where these bookshops will be found are Lille, Armentières, or Bethune.

The area is rural and places to dine are infrequent and not always open at expected hours.

If possible carry a packed picnic lunch and bottled water – don't forget a corkscrew for the wine – and remember to top up the fuel tank as opportunity arises.

Complementary to this guidebook, *The Battle of Neuve Chapelle* by

Tortuous sculpture in farmyard tub.

Geoff Bridger admirably covers in great detail the battle of 10 – 12 March 1915 mentioned only very briefly in this text by way of introduction, and details a thoroughly recommendable walking and touring guide around the earlier adjacent battlefield. Rose Coombs's book *Before Endeavours Fade* contains much information about the memorials and cemeteries in the surrounding area.

Having been too often lax through familiarity myself, may I advise you not to overlook the bare necessities. A small rucksack, bottled water and some refreshment, camera with spare films and batteries, a notebook and pencils, and waterproof footwear and clothing, are recommended. The area is flat and intensively farmed with tractors and farm traffic frequently using the lesser roads – the main routes are busy with hurrying cars and lorries and extra care is recommended. My experience is that the local farmers are very pleased to talk (in French) about their local knowledge and discoveries, and happy to help the numerous battlefield visitors. Do not trespass on private land or woods, avoid blocking field access, and do not dig for items. All kinds of munitions are still thrown up by ploughing and placed roadside to await removal by bomb disposal units. Do not touch them – the

90 years on, corroded, unstable, and dangerous. Each year large quantities are removed from verges by bomb disposal.

condition of old and corroded ammunition is unstable and the effect of sudden movements unpredictable – and possibly fatal.

The Commonwealth War Graves Commission, Maidenhead, Berks, may be contacted by telephone in the UK on 01628 634221, or their website can provide details of the whereabouts of those killed and buried in the area.

Remember to insure yourself and your car (a green copy of the International Motor Insurance Card obtainable from your insurer must be in your possession), and make sure your tetanus booster is up to date.

There are many hotels available within easy reach in Armentières, Bailleul, and Lille.

Those a little closer include;

Bethune: Hotel Le Vieux Beffroi, 48 Grand Place, 62400 Bethune.
Tel: (0033) 321 68 15 00
Beuvry: Formule 1, Rue Lamendin, Chemin de Teigneville, 62660
Beuvry: Tel: (0033) 321 64 19 19
Beuvry: Mister Bed, Rue Arthur Lemendin, 62660 Beuvry.
Tel: (0033) 321 65 95 95
Englos: Novotel Lille Englos, A25 Sortie Englos, 59320 Englos.
Tel: (0033) 320 10 58 58
Lestrem: La Cigogne, 256 Place de l'eglise, 62136 Lestrem.
Tel: (0033)321 02 57 77

Bed and Breakfast Gites de France accommodation in close proximity includes;

Benoit et Jacqueline Blondiaux Prins, 20 Rue de la Croix Barbée, 62136 Richebourg St Vaast Tel: (0033) 321 26 04 95
La Niche, Vielle - Chapelle, 62136 Richebourg
Tel: (0033) 321 65 33 13
Les Capcries, 106 Rue des Charbonniers, 62136 Richebourg
Tel: (0033) 321 26 07 19
La Pilaterie, 2129 rote d'Estaires, 62 La Couture
Tel: (0033) 321 26 77 02

As some gites open on a seasonal basis, prior reservation by telephone is necessary.

Websites giving information regarding tourist attractions and details of other other accommodation and events in the region are:
France Nord **www.cdt-nord.fr/** and Nord – Pas de Calais
www.northernfrance-tourism.com/

Chapter One

BACKGROUND OF EVENTS BEFORE THE BATTLE

After the sweep of the German advance across Belgium and northern France had been stemmed and the advance halted, the opposing lines of trenches and emplacements stretched from the Belgium coast through France to Switzerland. By 1915 the armies had become locked, opposing each other across the trench-lines, with combat restricted to raid-and-defend tactics. These, however brutal and fierce, were mainly punitive actions, grander British stratagems being restricted by a shortage of

Black Watch and Indians hold an important sector of the line near Fauquissart Post.

German soldiers train in the snow.

munitions, governed by restricted supplies and a lack of trained reserves, and military plans of the opposing armies were contained within the overall strategic political objectives of the protagonists.

Its part in the stemming of the rapid advance of the German army had severely depleted the British Expeditionary Force – the small but highly trained regular and reserve army had incurred very heavy casualties whilst being pushed back across Belgium and France. Replacement battalions from the territorial forces had been hurriedly re-kitted, brought to full readiness, and shipped over to bolster the fragile front line. Additional reserves were formed by mobilising older retired soldiers and reservists, and home based battalions and part trained recruits were pressed into active service. Many of the regular army battalions serving abroad, and additional fully trained troops and cavalry from the Indian regular army, were drafted from India to the European battlefronts. Arriving in the autumn of 1914 the Lahore and Meerut Divisions had to endure the particularly raw sub zero conditions of the harsh 1914/1915 winter, in waterlogged trenches on unfamiliar terrain, and under constant artillery bombardment. Engagement in the Neuve Chapelle attack and the Second Battle of Ypres severely depleted the number of regular officers and Indian soldiers. The standard of replacement recruits proved less capable, having been hurriedly selected and trained without particular regard to cultural backgrounds, and the morale and effectiveness of the Indian brigades had been certainly weakened.

Such was the position of the British armies at the time of the Aubers Ridge attack, before the battalions of the new army volunteers – Kitchener's Army – began to arrive at the front from mid 1915. In contrast the large German army was highly trained and well organised, having a General Staff without equal, and lead by very professional corps and staff officers who had absorbed more lessons from recent

conflicts. The ranks consisted of highly trained soldiers resulting from the system of compulsory military service, active reserve, and regular periods of refresher training, which had operated over many years since before the Franco Prussian War. A successful army career was regarded as the prime professional achievement in Germany, members of the armed forces and military excellence were highly respected and held in great esteem by the general population. The size and organisation of their army contrasted starkly with the smaller British equivalent which, although matching the German army in most disciplines, was outgunned and vastly inferior in medium and heavy artillery.

In Flanders the opposing armies were enmeshed in fierce combat around the bloody Ypres Salient in the continual struggles to capture and to defend that city, and the British in northern France were involved in a succession of vain attempts to breach the German line.

Actions near Givenchy and Cuinchy during January 1915 were followed by the ill-fated attack at Neuve Chapelle in March, then the double pronged assault against Aubers Ridge on May 9th preceded the Battle of Festubert, May 15th to 25th. A second attempt at Givenchy followed in mid June before the Battle of Loos and action at Hohenzollern Redoubt in September and October 1915.

The Battle of Aubers Ridge, supporting a larger French initiated offensive at Vimy, was the second of a linked trilogy of battles in the immediate area following shortly after the solely British attack known officially as the Battle of Neuve Chapelle (March 10th - 13th 1915) and whilst the 1915 Battle of Ypres, which had been raging on since 22 April, continued a few miles to the north.

The 1915 German strategic plan was to maintain the defence line on the western front whilst launching a major offensive against Russia, between Gorlice and Tarnow, to crush the Russian allied armies on the eastern front.

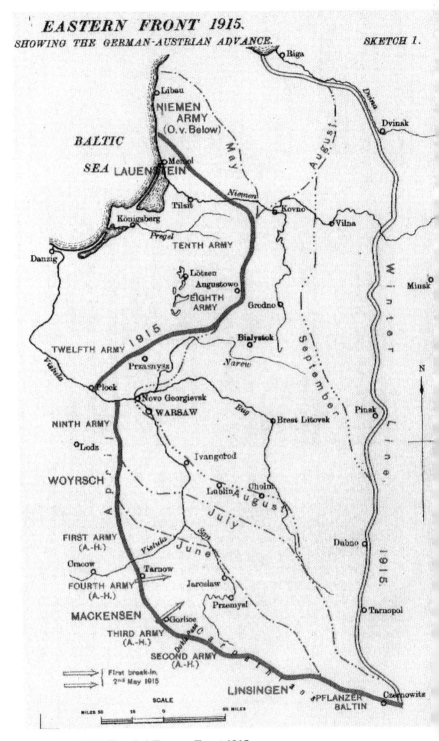

Map XXXX Sketch 1 Eastern Front 1915

General Erich von Falkenhayn, commander of the German army, had decided on the major offensive against Russia and, calculating that the French and British armies on the western front were incapable of effective penetrative action, ordered the withdrawal from the western front of 100,000 troops to strengthen the sixty-four divisions already arraigned along the eastern front.

General Joffre`s French plan for 1915 was to breach the German front by advancing northwards from the Verdun – Nancy line and from Rheims northwards to the Meziéres – Hirson railway; and to storm Vimy Ridge from the west.

General Erich von Falkenhayn.

The French army, which had incurred heavy losses in capturing part of the Notre Dame de Lorette spur at the north end of Vimy Ridge in December 1914 and, early in 1915 had lost another 50,000 men without effective gain in Champagne, suffered the loss of a further 64,000 men in the fruitless and pointless attack against the German salient at St Mihiel.

However, the French Army high command at this time was still firmly convinced that, in spite of the very heavy cumulative losses, the large army at their disposal, properly marshalled, had sufficient trained infantrymen, artillery firepower and the will, to break through the German defence line and expel the invaders from France.

General Joffre and General Foch, commanding the northern army, enthusiastically planned to throw the full weight of their forces against the German defences guarding the Douai plain, and thus to break through and cut the Valenciennes – Douai rail supply lines which serviced the three German Armies active on the western front, thereby forcing withdrawal.

General Joffre.

As part of this plan Sir John French, commanding the British Forces, was requested to partake in a joint attack on La Bassée. This request was declined, as was the additional suggestion that the British take over the

21

General Foch.

Sir John French.

Bombardment of Neuve Chapelle.

line to the north of Ypres to release French forces. Neither liking the French commanders nor being regarded in high esteem by them, mutually antagonistic attitudes between the British and French high commands had developed which resulted in the relationship, by early 1915, being decidedly sour.

General Joffre, upset by what he regarded as the pompous British attitude, postponed his offensive in the north and suggested that the British mount their own offensive.

Sir John French did decide to mount an attack against the salient at Neuve Chapelle and on 15 Feb 1915 instructed Haig, commander of his First Army, to draw up plans. On 2 March, in correspondence with Rawlinson, commanding IV Army Corps, Haig described his conception of the plan

> *Our objective is not merely the capture of Neuve Chapelle.*
> *Our existing line [is] just as satisfactory for us as if we were in*
> *Neuve Chapelle. I aim getting to the line of the La Bassée road*
> *to Lille and thus cut off the enemy's front. It seems to me*
> *desirable to make our plan in the chance of surprising the enemy*
> *and with the definite objective of advancing rapidly (and without*
> *any check) in the hope of starting a general advance.*

This plan, which would be the first full scale attack by the British against a properly established German trench system, failed to recognise the waste of pitting cavalry against machine guns and did not take into account the German defensive strategy of siting heavy machine gun posts behind their front lines to break up any rapid mounted advance.

At 7.30 am on 10 March 1915 a barrage of thirty minutes duration, limited in both intensity and time, ammunition being in short supply due to the serious difference between need and the production capacity of the certified suppliers, battered the German trench system fronting Neuve Chapelle. Immediately following the bombardment the British launched a fourteen-battalion strong attack against the six German companies and twelve machine guns defending the village.

A successful breakthrough at the centre of the attack front foundered when uncut wire and heavy enfilade machine gunfire from the cleverly sited Maxim guns arrested movement on the flanks, causing serious congestion which prevented the effective forward movement of reserves. The momentum of the initial advance ground to a standstill and, although the British attempted in vain to renew the advance over the following three days, repeated German counter attacks pushed them back to within 800 metres of their starting line.

IWM Q35446

The German Maxim Machine gun. Cleverly sited and used to deadly effect at Neuve Chapelle and Aubers Ridge.

Without any meaningful gain the British had incurred 12,900 casualties.

Rawlinson, an infantryman, wrote immediately afterwards:

I think DH [Haig] would have been better advised to content himself with the capture of the village instead of going on with the attack on 11th 12th and 13th for the purpose of trying to get the cavalry through. I advised him to do this in the first instance but he and Sir John [French] were so obsessed with the cavalry idea that he would not listen. Had he been content with the village we should have gained just as much ground and reduced our casualties by three-quarters.

However the dour ruling military minds of the time accepted the limited success at Neuve Chapelle with great optimism. The debriefing of the failure, so costly and wasteful in human lives and resources, viewed the events very positively. Inexperience in mobilising reserves, the sparse artillery, and the shortage of ammunition, were allegedly the reasons for not capitalising on the initial breakthrough, which in turn prevented the mounted cavalry from attacking through the gap to storm German second line positions.

The official conclusion was that with more guns and sufficient shells to cause a wrecking barrage, and with larger reserves operated across a broader front to allow an unhampered flow of follow up troops, this pattern of assault would, without doubt, unstoppably breach the German defences.

Haig stated in a letter to Rothschild:

I think the main lesson of Neuve Chapelle is that, given sufficient ammunition and suitable guns, we can break through the enemy's line whenever we like!

Also impressed by the ease of the initial breakthrough by the British troops at Neuve Chapelle, at the end of March a less antagonistic General Joffre approached Sir John French again to suggest that the British be involved in supporting a planned French assault on the German front line. A major attack against Vimy Ridge in early May would, he suggested, be greatly assisted by the British simultaneously attacking again in the area of Neuve Chapelle.

The objective of the Joffre plan was to capture Vimy Ridge and advance across the plain of Douai beyond. By attacking with the full force of the French Tenth Army – fourteen infantry divisions, 750 pieces of field artillery and over 200 heavy guns, all under the command of General d'Urbal, to occupy the high ridge between Farbus and Souchez – the French army would command the lower ground of the plain situated below these heights, from where it could advance to capture the industrial areas of Lens and Douai and onward against the Cambrai - Douai line.

The operational plan was to capture the eastern spur of Notre Dame de Lorette, on the left flank, during the day preceding the main assault, and to launch another subsidiary attack, simultaneous with the British attack at Neuve Chapelle, on the day after the main assault. These additional attacks were designed to extend the breach and to deter any movement of enemy reserves from north of the La Bassée Canal which could counterattack the main French thrust.

Having advised General Foch that his First Army would support the French attack towards Vimy Ridge by undertaking an offensive against the German front in the area of Neuve Chapelle, Sir John French issued his orders from the British Advanced Headquarters at Hazebrouck on 4th May.

The First Army will take the offensive on 8th May. Its mission is to break through the enemy's line on its front and gain the La Bassée – Lille road between La Bassée and Fournes. Its further advance will be directed on the line Bauvin – Don. The Cavalry Corps, Indian Cavalry Corps, Canadian Division, Highland [51st] Division (less one brigade R.F.A.) and Northumbrian [50th] Division will be in general reserve at the disposal of the Field Marshal, and will be ready to move at two hours notice.

In fact, the Canadian Division and the Northumbrian Division had been severely affected by losses at Ypres during the last week of April and the 51st Division had not yet arrived in France.

After consultation, the imperturbable General Sir Douglas Haig, commander of the British First Army, confidently planned his part in the operation. By means of a pincer movement he would secure Aubers Ridge and sever the La Bassée to Lille road – a vital artery in the German supply route.

Aubers Ridge is hardly worth the name. The ridge is barely 20 metres in height – a mere crease in the flat lands of Northern France – but in the context of the flat waterlogged battleground of 1915, criss-crossed by deep drainage ditches and innumerable dykes, occupation of this slightly elevated ground gave a huge advantage to the defenders of the German positions, overlooking Neuve Chapelle, Festubert, and the opposing front lines.

The advancing German forces in 1914 had been able to choose the most favourable contours and to utilise the higher ground within their forward positions to engineer formidable strong points and had, since the battle at Neuve Chapelle, worked to strengthen their defences considerably across this whole front.

After what was described in their official records as the 'almost disastrous Neuve Chapelle engagement', the German Army Command had issued engineering orders to strengthen the defence works along the Aubers Ridge and had increased troop density – from two to three divisions – under the Corps Command of General von Claer. On 20 March, having rested in reserve after the battle of Neuve Chapelle, four regiments of the 6th Bavarian Reserve Division took over from the 13th Division the 9000 metre wide sector between Bois Grenier at the northern extreme and Fauquissart. The three regiments of the 13th Division were concentrated between Fauquissart and Chocolat Menier Corner, some 8000 metres, and the adjoining three regiments of the 14th Division covered another 8000 metres from Chocolat Menier Corner to Cuinchy. Each regiment held about 2500 metres of front instead of 3500 metres as before the Neuve Chapelle battle – which had been regarded by the German High Command as uncomfortably close to a disastrous British breakthrough. The increase in troop density thus effected, quickly allowed a release of more working parties to increase the strength of the defences. The duty roster was that each company served six days in the front trench, two days in support, and four days in reserve rest billets. The companies in rest billets provided, with additional squads from training depots at Wavrin and Lille, night working parties to supplement those in the front line

German signals station, Aubers Ridge, 1919.

IWM Q37

on construction duties. The digging of suitable conventional trenches being impossible due to the high water table (less than a metre below the surface), the parapets and parados forming the defensive breastworks were greatly increased in both height and depth using sandbags. The parapets were increased to five to seven metres in width and two metres in height. The ditches fronting the parapets, formed by the excavation of soil used in the construction, were filled with coiled barbed wire, and the entanglements fronting these ditches were widened and strengthened using heavy gauge barbed wire.

Within the breastworks, reckoned by the German engineers to be capable of withstanding all but the very heaviest of available British armament, formidable fire points were constructed. Every few metres large wooden boxes at ground level, each designed to shelter two riflemen, were built into the facing and protected by sandbags up to the height of the parapet and also, near to ground level and set twenty metres apart, large V shaped wooden boxes were similarly built into the walls to serve as machine gun emplacements. The guns, capable of sweeping through a wide arc, fired through steel-rail loopholes. Higher concentrations of fire points of extra strength were constructed at bends in the line and salients, to form strong points from which troops advancing towards the main front could be subjected to enfilade fire on either flank. In addition to the built in emplacements, screened emplacements were built in front of the barbed wire defences with shallow access trenches to enable gunners to crawl out to man the posts in the event of attack. The second line, some 200 metres behind the front, and the linking communication trenches were also greatly strengthened, fire steps were cut, and much was roofed with hurdles or canvas screens to conceal movement of men and material. By the end of April all the scheduled engineering work had been completed.

With two German divisions in reserve, the fortifications now stood as a formidable barrier against which the attacking British, although much

German trench – 1915.

27

superior in number, would be pitted.

The British offensives of 1915 suffered chronic and severely disrupting shortages of guns and ammunition. The supply policy existing at the time limited ammunition production to the Royal Ordnance factories and a few accredited suppliers under War Office direction. This supply principle was being jealously guarded by the Master General of Ordnance at the War Office, Major-General Sir Stanley von Donop, with the parsimonious collusion of Lord Kitchener. Appeals to increase output by using extra available industrial capacity were being stoutly resisted despite the repeated urgent demands by Sir John French, the Commander in Chief of the BEF, for substantial increases in supplies of shells and heavy guns for the western front.

Shortly before the battle, Lieutenant-Colonel DH Drake-Brockman, commanding the 39th Gharwalis in trenches fronting Aubers Ridge, wrote:

> *If one telephoned up to the gunner officer for a little ammunition to be expended on some bomb gun or minenwerfer that was annoying us, the reply generally received was, 'Sorry, but I have used my allowance!'*

This, at the time, was eighteen rounds per battery per day.

Under considerable political pressure from Lloyd George and James Balfour, leader of the Conservative Party, the then Prime Minister, Asquith, set up a 'Munitions of War' cabinet committee to investigate and instigate measures to solve the problem of supply shortages. Despite great efforts by Churchill and Lloyd George to promote the use of new sources radically to increase ammunition output, continuing resistance, particularly from Lord Kitchener, the appointed committee chairman, frustrated all efforts to achieve the necessary increased targets for shell production, although the outside purchase of some additional quantities of armaments was agreed.

In early April 1915 Sir John French met with Lord Kitchener at the War Office personally to press earlier demands for the vitally necessary increases in ammunition supplies. Whether by mistake or design, and much to the fury of Sir John French, in a letter to Asquith dated 14th April 1915 Kitchener stated:

> *I have had a talk with French. He told me I could let you know that with the present supply of ammunition he will have as much as his troops will be able to use on the next forward movement.*

On the basis of this information Asquith denied press reports of inadequate armament and shell supplies. Bearing in mind the continual and increasingly frantic appeals for increases from Sir John French, his anger on hearing of the incident must have been extreme. He was convinced that his words had been deliberately misinterpreted and his feelings on the matter were conveyed to the War Office supremo in no uncertain terms.

On being informed by Sir John French that no increase could be expected, Haig did suggest a temporary transfer of guns from the Second Army. The Second Battle of Ypres, which had flared into action following the German gas attack of 22 April 1915 and would continue until 25 May, prevented any such solution.

On 1st May the tally of guns available for the attack was:

Heavy Artillery : Howitzers.

15 inch	3
4.7 inch – quick firing (obsolete)	28
5 inch – (obsolete)	20
6 inch Mk 7 breech loader	40
60 pdr breech loader	20
9.2 inch Mk 10 breech loader	10

Field Artillery : light guns and Howitzers.

13 pdr Quick firing	84
18 pdr Quick firing (standard)	276
4.5 inch Quick firing	60
15 pdr breech loader (obsolete)	84

In 1914 the Royal Field Artillery (RFA) served the infantry and the Royal Horse Artillery (RHA) supported the cavalry. The RHA as standard used 18-pdrs (3.3 in) and quick firing 13-pdrs (3 in), the RFA using quick firing 18-pdrs and the 4.5 inch howitzers which had been

designed as weapons to destroy fixed fortifications and strong points. The howitzer fired low velocity heavy shells with a high trajectory and relatively short range, the field guns firing higher velocity lower trajectory missiles over longer distances. Dependable fuses and chemical sophistication had not been sufficiently developed by the British to produce fully efficient high explosive (HE) shells for general use, a deficiency which would be cruelly exposed during the battle.

The British Expeditionary Force commander at the time of the Aubers Ridge offensive was Field Marshal Sir John French, his Army commanders being the then General Sir Douglas Haig, First Army, holding Cuichy to Bois Grenier (including Aubers Ridge), and General Sir Horace Smith-Dorien, Second Army, the Ypres area.

The First Army Order of Battle Aubers Ridge 1915 under General Haig was:

General Staff

Br.- [Major] General, — Brigadier-General RHK Butler
DA and QMG — Brigadier-General PEF Hobbs
Major-General, Royal Artillery — Major-General HF Mercer
Chief Engineer — Major-General SR Rice

I Corps

Commander — Lieutenant-General Sir CC Monro
Br. General — Brigadier-General RD Whigham
DA and QMG — Brigadier-General HN Sargent
Br. General, Royal Artillery — Brigadier-General RAK Montgomery
Chief Engineer — Brigadier-General C Godby

1st Division

Commander — Major-General RCB Haking

1 (Guards) Brigade — Brigadier-General HC Lowther
1/Coldstream Guards — 1/Black Watch 1/14 London (London Scottish)
1/Scots Guards — 1/Camerons

2 Brigade — Brigadier-General GH Thesiger
2/Royal Sussex — 1/Loyal N. Lancs 1/9 King's Liverpool (TF)
1/Northants — 2/KRRC 1/5 Royal Sussex (TF)

3 Brigade — Brigadier-General HR Davies
1/South Wales Borderers — 2/Welsh 1/4 Royal Welsh Fusiliers
1/Gloucesters — 2/Royal Munster Fusiliers

RFA Brigades

XXV (114, 115, 118 Btys)   XXVI (116, 117 Btys)
XXXIX (46, 51, 54 Btys)
Field Companies RE 23, 26, 1/1st Lowland (TF)
Mounted Troops : B Sqdn Northumberland Hussars (Yeo) Cyclist Coy

2nd Division
Commander   Major General HS Horne

IV Corps
Commander   Lieutenant-General Sir HS Rawlinson
DA and QMG   Brigadier-General AG Dallas
Brigadier General RA   Brigadier-General AH Hussey
Chief Engineer   Brigadier-General RUH Buckland

7th Division
Commander
Major-General H de la P Gough

20 Brigade	Brigadier-General FJ Heyworth
1/Grenadier Guards	2/Border 1/6 Gordon Highlanders
2/Scots Guards	2/Gordons

21 Brigade	Brigadier-General GE Watts
2/Bedfordshire	2/Royal Scots Fus 1/4 Camerons(TF)
2/Green Howards	2/Wiltshire

22 Brigade	Brigadier-General STB Lawford
2/Queen's	1/R Welch Fus 1/8 R Scots(TF)
2/R Warwicks	1/South Staffs

RHA Bde XIV (F & T Btys)
RFA Bde XXII (104, 105, 106 Btys) XXXV (12, 25, 58 Btys)
55 Bty of XXXVII (How) Bde
Field Companies RE : 54, 55, & 1/2 Highland (TF)
Mounted Troops : HQ & A Sqdn Northumberland Hussars (Yeo.) Cyclist Coy

8th Division
Commander   Major-General FJ Davies

23 Brigade	Brigadier-General RJ Pinney
2/Devonshire	2/Scottish Rifles 1/6 Scottish Rifles (TF)
2/West Yorks	2/Middlesex 1/7 Middlesex (TF)

24 Brigade	Brigadier-General RS Oxley
2/East Lancs	2/Northants
	1/Notts and Derbys (Sherwood Foresters)
1/Worcesters	1/5 Black Watch (TF)

25 Brigade	Brigadier-General AWG Lowry Cole
2/Lincolnshire	1/Royal Irish Rifles 1/1 London (TF)
2/Royal Berks	2/Rifle Brigade 1/13 London (TF)

RHA Bde	V (O & Z Btys)
RFA Bdes	XXXIII (32, 33, 36 Btys)
	XXXVII (How) (31 & 35 Btys)
	XLV (1, 3, 5 Btys)
Field Companies RE:	2, 15, & 1/1 Home Counties (TF)
Mounted Troops:	C Sqdn Northumberland Hussars (Yeo.)
	Cyclist Coy

Indian Corps

Commander	Lieutenant-General Sir J Willcocks
Brigadier General, General Staff	Brigadier-General H Hudson
DA & QMG	Brigadier-General AS Cobbe
Brigadier General RA	Brigadier-General AB Scott
Chief Engineer	Brigadier-General HC Nanton

Meerut Division

Commander	Lieutenant-General Sir CA Anderson
Dehra Dun Brigade	Brigadier-General CW Jacob
2/2 Gurkhas	6 Jats 1/4 Seaforths (TF)
1/9 Gurkhas	1/Seaforth Highlanders
Garhwal Brigade	Brigadier-General CG Blackader
2/Leicesters	2/3 Gurkhas 1/3 London (TF)
39/Garhwal Rifles	2/8 Gurkhas
Bareilly Brigade	Brigadier-General WM Southey
2/Black Watch	58th Vaughan's Rifles
	1/4 BlackWatch (TF)
41st Dogras	125th Napier's Rifles
RFA Bdes	IV (7, 14, 66 Btys) XIII (2, 8, 44 Btys)
	IX (19, 20, 28 Btys)
	XLIII (How) Bde (30 Bty)
Engineers	1st Sappers and Miners (3 & 4 Coys)
Pioneers	107 Pioneers

Lahore Division

Commander	Major-General H D'U Keary

Royal Flying Corps

1st Wing	Lieutenant-Colonel HM Trenchard
2, 3, & 16 Squadrons	

German Order of Battle Aubers Ridge 1915

Sixth Army (Part)

Commander	Crown Prince Rupprecht of Bavaria
Chief of Staff	Major-General Krafft von Delmensingen
VII Corps	General von Claer
13th Division	Lieutenant-General von dem Borne
25th Brigade	13th and 158th Regiments
26th Brigade	15th and 55th Regiments
14th Division	Lieutenant-General von Ditfurth
27th Brigade	16th and 53rd Regiments
79th Brigade	56th and 57th Regiments
Corps Troops	11th Jager Battalion
6th Bavarian Reserve Division	Lieutenant-General von Scanzoni
12th Bavarian Res Bgde	16th and 17th Bavarian Reserve Regts
14th Bavarian Res Bgde	9th 20th & 21st Bavarian Reserve Regts

Chapter Two

PLANS AND PREPARATION

During April the First Army front facing Neuve Chapelle had been re-organised. The Indian Corps relieved I Corps of the 1500 yards wide front between the Orchard Redoubt (1300 yards north of Chocolat Menier Corner) and Neuve Chapelle, and the 47th (London) Division took over the 600 yard south end of the front between Cuinchy and Chocolat Menier Corner, thus enabling I Corps to assemble the 2nd Division as reserve behind the 1st Division which was to be concentrated on an attack front of some 1300 yards width.

Abutting the 1st Division, the Meerut Division of the Indian Corps was assembled on an 800 yards wide attack front, and the Lahore Division, much reduced after having assisted the Second Army fight in the battle of Ypres during the last week of April, took over the remainder of the front line up to Neuve Chapelle.

Similarly, on IV Corps front 49 (West Riding) Division took over most of the front whilst 8th Division amassed forces along the allotted assault front of 1500 yards astride the Sailly – Fromelles road, with 7th Division behind in reserve.

A successful breakthrough by the assaulting infantry battalions depended upon an artillery bombardment effectively disabling the opposing fortifications despite the restrictions of limited shell supply. Across terrain not favoured by artillery, flat land with little natural cover, a short 'surprise' bombardment was planned – by necessity rather than choice. Against the Vimy Ridge objectives to the south the French artillery had bombarded for five days using 300 heavy calibre guns and nearly 1000 others, but the British had no more guns per square yard of front available than they had for the inconclusive attack at Neuve Chapelle two months earlier.

The commanders of the HAR (Heavy Artillery Reserve) Groups and the Divisional Artillery allotted specific tasks and targets to each battery within the forty minute preliminary bombardment. The low trajectory 18 pdrs and light batteries would be concentrated on wire cutting for the first ten minutes of the barrage then lift to join the rest of the guns pounding the enemy breastworks, whilst the 13 pdrs concentrated fire behind the enemy lines to isolate their front line trenches and to impede any forward movement of reinforcements. In fact the only available guns capable of inflicting appreciable damage to

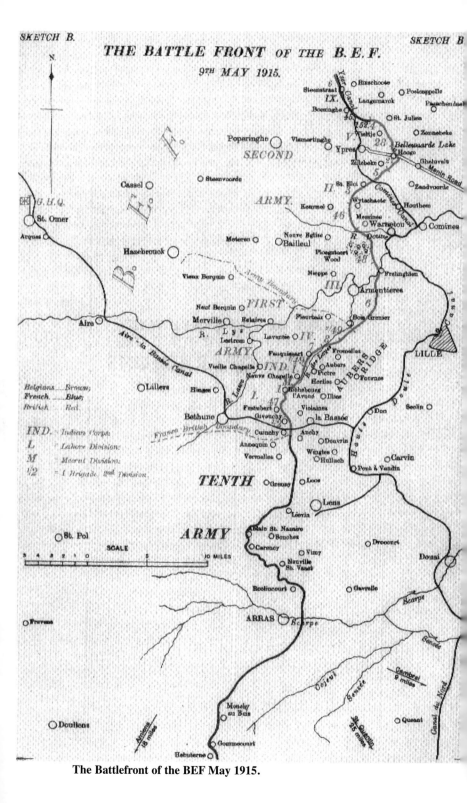

The Battlefront of the BEF May 1915.

the breastworks and breaking through parapets were the 60 pdrs and 9.2 inch guns of the HAR, of which a mere eighteen were serviceable. They had been detailed to destroy the fortified strong points at Cour d`Avoue Farm and Deleval Farm.

General Haig had counter proposed to Sir John French that, instead of the single attack to the south of Neuve Chapelle as originally suggested by General Foch, a two pronged attack be launched to break through both to the north and the south of the village. From the two intrusions the breached German line would then be rolled back to connect into a wide front through which heavy reserve forces would advance. The essence of the plan was that following the encirclement of the German positions, under the direction of the local commanders, a rapid advance would be effected on successive points stretching nine kilometers on from Aubers Ridge to the Heute Deule canal. Reserves would pour through behind to consolidate the gains.

The First Army, under the command of General Haig, comprised I Corps including the Indian Army Corps, and IV Corps. Commanding I Corps was Lieutenant-General Sir CC Munro, an old friend and close confidant of Haig. The Indian Army Corps was under the command of the gentlemanly, overweight, and much caricatured, General Sir James Willcocks, and the IV Army Corps commanded by the very capable Lieutenant-General Sir Henry Rawlinson.

Reports from military intelligence and Royal Flying Corps reconnaissance had, since the beginning of April, repeatedly relayed details of the extensive work underway on strengthening defences and of increasing troop and armament density. Haig, no doubt encouraged by the sudden optimism of the French army command, chose to overlook or ignore the threats posed by these changes and proceeded with his preconceived plan of attack based on the breakthrough at Neuve Chapelle in March, totally convinced that the pressure of his superior numbers would this time ensure complete breakthrough and success.

General Sir James Willcocks

Lieutenant-General Sir Henry Rawlinson

Rawlinson added his own concern regarding specific newly constructed strong points, and the extensive dugouts, but Haig still recognised no need to amend his plan, displaying the traits of stubbornness, inflexibility and self belief, which would be often and expensively repeated throughout the course of the war.

Taking into consideration the lessons learned during the battle at Neuve Chapelle, preparations and specialist training for the attack pressed urgently ahead during the four weeks prior to the planned zero hour. The flat forward areas, devoid of adequate cover and crossed by water filled ditches aplenty, were visited and reconnoitred by officers of the assaulting infantry battalions. Approach routes were improved, new trenches dug, and abandoned trenches in No Man`s Land were renovated ready for use as forward assault exits. Rows of assembly trenches were constructed behind the front line trenches to shelter the follow up troops, breastworks were built up and additional step portes cut to enable a rapid and unbunched deployment of attackers. Ammunition and supply dumps and engineers stores were sited, built and stocked, and gun emplacements constructed. Although activity was carried out with as much secrecy as was possible the suspicion of the defenders was manifested only in extra artillery activity but, in spite of additional losses, the work of the engineers and pioneers progressed in accordance to plan. Surprisingly no official entry noting detection of these widespread activities appear in German field diaries before 8 May. During the night preceding the battle, additional quantities of short ladders were erected against the parapets to supplement the exit portes and steps, light bridges were placed across ditches and dykes in front of the breastworks, and pathways cut through the wire to allow the advancing troops an unhindered exit.

A heavy and prolonged thunderstorm on 4 May heralded days of hot and humid weather and regular heavy showers, filling the ditches and returning the drying ground to cloying mud.

British tunnelling techniques had been rapidly developing under the energetic inspiration of Major Norton Griffiths MP. In civilian life a contractor specialising in the construction of underground sewers, his enthusiasm had inspired the quick creation of the Royal Engineers tunnelling companies. On the Rouges Bancs front two mine galleries seventy yards apart, one 283 feet, the other 330 ft in length, had been deep dug through the subsoil of blue clay by 173 Tunnelling Company RE, each charged with 2000lbs of explosive under the stretch of German front line trench due to be attacked by the 1/13 London Regiment. German miners had abandoned attempts to tunnel in the opposite direction due to the amount of surface water.

The infantry, 8th Division of IV Corps in the north and 1st Division of I Corps plus the Meerut Division of the Indian Army in the south, having pierced the enemy defences, would rush the breaches, fight and bomb along the ridge in a pincer movement to trap the defenders, and thus open the way for mass advance along the whole of the front thus exposed.

Trenches on this part of the front, flat ground with a high water table, were very shallow with built up frontal and rear breastworks. The German defensive breastworks had been greatly increased in height and depth, and the ancillary fortifications and infrastructure had been strengthened accordingly. The sandbags used as facings in the construction of the breastworks, black, white, and various hues of brown, very effectively camouflaged the position of the many fire holes cleverly designed into the structure.

In terms of arms and position the German army was undoubtedly superior, but in numbers the attacking British and Indian troops far exceeded the defenders.

Although the British Lee Enfield rifles had proved better in performance than the German Gewehr 98, in other areas German armaments were more effective. Grenades available to the German infantryman at that time were threefold and dependable. The standard hand grenade, cylindrical and packed with explosive, was fitted with a short time fuse simply activated by pulling a cord running through the hollow tubular throwing handle. In addition the foot soldiers carried small egg grenades, and what were known as 'pineapples' – small grenades with iron cases divided into segments which upon explosion scattered into deadly fragments. All had an effective range of about 45 metres. Minenwerfers – 25 cm trench mortars – known to the British soldiers as 'moaning minnies', hurled destructive black drums packed with 200 pounds of explosive into enemy positions. The German army, most significantly, was equipped with large numbers of Maxim heavy machine guns and was thoroughly and specifically trained to utilise the weapon to maximum killing effect.

Their Field Artillery was armed with 'whizz bangs', 7.7 cm field

German bomber with four grenades for trench to trench action.

37

The traditional pickelhauber helmet was worn as combat headgear by the defenders, although the 'spike' was usually removed and the helmet covered in canvas.

guns which fired 15lb shells and 10.5 cm howitzers, and the Foot Artillery were armed with 15 cm and 21 cm howitzers – these fired devastatingly effective HE shells which exploded in clouds of dense black smoke, and were nicknamed by their recipients as 'coal boxes' or 'Jack Johnsons', after the reigning world heavyweight boxing champion of the time. The German artillery batteries suffered no supply restrictions and were amply provisioned with good quality ammunition.

Haig's armies, under the direction of their general and in accordance with his preconceived plan for the breakthrough which he held in supreme and unshakeable confidence, would attack against this array of carefully sited weaponry, vastly improved defences, and troop and armament density much increased since the Neuve Chapelle battle.

The Mills bomb and the Stokes mortar would soon be introduced to remedy the British deficiencies in arms but neither was available for use at the time of the Aubers Ridge engagement. The traditional pickelhauber helmet was worn as headgear by the defenders – picturesque certainly – but more protective than the cloth hats worn at the time by the British Tommy. Not until the early part of 1916 would steel helmets become available to both armies as standard headgear.

After a 40 minutes long artillery bombardment, the brigades leading the attack fronts some 6,000 yards apart would advance and occupy the opposing front line trenches, then move forward to capture their next tactical objectives. Meeting in a pincer movement from the north and the south of Neuve Chapelle and uniting into a single continuous attack front, the troops following up would then rapidly advance to occupy positions on Aubers Ridge one and a half miles ahead.

The stronger southern attack would be undertaken by 1st Division and the Meerut Division of the Indian Corps advancing side by side on a front 2,400 yards wide between Chocolat Menier Corner and the British strong point at Port Arthur.

The Meerut Division, on the left flank of this attack, would then advance in a north easterly direction to capture La Cliqueterie Farm, situated one and a half miles behind the existing front, which had been recently fortified and transformed by the Germans into a formidable fortress.

The northern attack led by 8th Division would, immediately after breakthrough, move rapidly south eastwards towards Rouge Bancs and establish a front running along the Sailly to Fromelles road, thence to Aubers, and on to link up with the Meerut Division at La Cliqueterie Farm.

Six German regiments along a three-mile front would thus be contained within the pincer trap. Troops from IV Corps and the Indian Corps were detailed to secure the strategic points of Aubers village and La Russie farm at the north east corner of the Bois du Biez, to capture the guns, and to neutralise the surrounded German forces. After consolidation of the new line along Aubers Ridge, reserve brigades and artillery would be moved forward to effect the second phase of the planned action – a further seven kilometer advance to the Haute Deule canal.

Three squadrons of twin seater BE2 biplanes of the 1st Wing of the Royal Flying Corps, under the command of Lieutenant-Colonel HM Trenchard, were attached to First Army and flew defensive patrols for four days before the battle to stop any attempts by the German air corps to carry out aerial reconnaissance. During the battle at least one aeroplane was to be airborne at all times and, from an operational altitude of 4000 feet, report back, via an experimental wireless telegraphy link, as to troop positions. White linen strips size seven feet by two feet were to be rolled out to indicate the position of the lead assault troops, and artillery observers were to receive pinpoint information regarding enemy positions. On the day few strips were unrolled and the 42 messages relayed to the ground proved useless, as the observers were neither able to identify points nor to distinguish British from German troops across the flat featureless terrain. Various objectives of strategic importance were to be bombed –

Lieutenant-Colonel HM Trenchard.

The BE2 was the workhorse of the RFC and flew defensive patrols before the battle to stop German aerial reconnaissance.

although bombing techniques were primitive. To stay the forward movement of supplies, the villages of Illies, Herlies, Fournes, and Marquillies, and the rail and road bridges over the canal at Don (eight kilometers north-east of La Bassée), were specified as targets. Additional bombing raids were to be carried out by HQ Wing RFC on rail junctions to the south east and north of Lille, on the railway stations at Seclin, Tournai and Roubaix, and on the German High Command HQ. None of the specified targets were hit.

Zero hour was first scheduled to be at 5.40 am on Saturday 8 May 1915, the day following the main French attack at Vimy. However, heavy rain on the Thursday was followed by thick mist, adversely affecting the artillery programmes, and General d'Urbal, as a result, rescheduled his main attack, firstly to the Saturday and finally decided that the attacks should all take place together on Sunday 9 May. Circumstances had at least fulfilled Sir John French's wishes for his army attack to be simultaneous with the French attack at Vimy. The unexpected delay caused some consternation in the keyed up British ranks when action was postponed at the very moment of departure to battle stations. Haig, now in his advanced HQ at Merville, received notice of the delayed French zero hour only at 5 pm on the Friday and, by the time the relayed information had been received by some battalions, packs and blankets had already been dumped and the troops assembled ready for the forward move in battle order. Thankfully, as they waited, although chill, the night remained fine.

The battered church tower at Laventie, appropriated as the most suitable position close to IV Corps HQ from which to survey the forthcoming battle, was used by Sir John French and party as viewing post. Winston Churchill, at the time First Lord of the Admiralty and a close friend of Sir John, on breaking his journey at St Omer on his way back from Paris where he had been attending a meeting with his French and Italian equivalents, had learned of the impending engagement and decided to join Sir John and his staff in their vantage point to watch the battle progress.

On the afternoon of 7 May news of the sinking by a German submarine off the coast of Ireland of the Atlantic liner *Lusitania* with the loss of 2000 passengers and crew had been received. This sudden shocking change in the sea war tactics outraged public and, definitively, American opinion.

Chapter Three

BOMBARDMENT & ATTACK

On the southern front the four lead battalions of 2 and 3 Brigades of the 1st Division crossed the Rue du Bois up into the front trenches with, on their left, the three lead battalions of the Dehra Dun Brigade. The assault battalions behind the front and second breastworks, with support battalions in the Gridiron trenches behind the Rue du Bois ready to move forward into the attack trenches as the assaulting troops went over the parapets.

On the northern sector front, the lead battalions of 24 and 25 Brigades of 8th Division faced Rouges Bancs ready to attack. 23 Brigade moved into divisional reserve positions fronting Rue Tilleloy at Petillon, and 7th Division waited in general reserve to the west of Petillon. By 2.30 am on the clear cloudless night of Sunday 9th May, all troops were assembled in their forward positions.*

*See Appendix 1 First Army Operation order No 22 p180

The forward trenches became increasingly overcrowded as the attacking battalions joined those holding the line. The varied and cluttering amount of assault equipment – ladders to scale the parapet and planks and foot ladders for crossing ditches, extra ammunition, bombs and shovels, all added to the crush of troops in battle order.

During the starlit Saturday night all remained quiet on the opposing German front. Fortified by a rum and tea issue the troops settled and awaited in silence for the break of dawn at 4 am and then, at 5 am, the bursting of the artillery barrage to herald the attack. Trained and poised, ready to crawl forward under the screaming shells, the shrill blasts of subalterns' whistles would signal the order to troops to rise and cross No Man's Land, to overcome the enemy and remove him from his trenches.

At 5 am the silence along the two fronts was abruptly shattered as six hundred British guns burst into action with a deafening roar.

Wattle and earth – British Breastworks along the Rue du Bois – 1915. IWM Q⁵

Trench dig – Rue Petillon May 1915.

Raging explosions, and sheets of orange and yellow flames flashed amongst a pall of black and grey cloud as the barrage of shells burst upon the trenches opposite, obliterating the view and causing the very ground to tremble beneath the feet of the thousands poised to attack. With visibility obscured by smoke and debris, for the first ten minutes of the barrage the field guns bombarded the enemy barbed wire defences with shrapnel shells, then lifted to join the other artillery in pounding the German breastwork and trenches. For a brief interlude a swirling breeze cleared the view to expose a glimpse of the enemy already manning their parapets in spite of the terrible blanket of shellfire raining around them, pickelhaubers and bayonets glinting ominously, rifles cocked at the ready and waiting for attackers to emerge.

The billowing smoke and dust, which obscured visibility over the flat terrain, prevented Forward Observation officers of the Royal Artillery from accurately directing fire from their batteries. In the confusion of the battle messages relayed back to Nos 1 and 2 Group

HAR from the BE2 reconnaissance planes circling above failed to pinpoint strategic targets. To add to these shortcomings, due to faulty ammunition and worn barrels, a considerable quantity of shells were falling short – particularly the 4.7inch shells targeted on the German rear batteries. The copper driving bands were stripping off as the shells left the muzzles and the tumbling shells, erratic in direction, fell randomly short, inflicting losses amongst the closely packed British assault troops.

A. DAWN ATTACK – 1st DIVISION from the Rue du Bois (Southern Front)

*See
Appendix 2
I Corps
Operation
Order No79
pp181

*See
Appendix 3
I Division
Order No81
pp182

On the First Army front, 1st Division, under the command of Major-General RCB Haking, opened the attack, whilst 2nd Division, in support, under Major-General HS Horne, moved up to within three miles of the front. The 47th Division, commanded by Major-General CStL Barter, which held the line to the south of the attack, was to move over after the breakthrough to take over captured ground from 1st Division and to occupy the Rue d'Ouvert, one mile east of Festubert.

General Haking's 1st Division HQ was set up in a ruined house in the Rue du Bois. The four assault battalions of his 2 and 3 Brigades were positioned along the 1600 yards wide front between Chocolat Menier Corner and Orchard Redoubt, the two brigades divided by the cart track which served the Ferme du Bois.

Brigadier-General EA Fanshawe, the artillery commander, operated from Divisional HQ, whilst 2 Brigade (Brigadier-General GH Thesinger) and 3 Brigade (Brigadier-General HR Davies) also established separate headquarters in ruined but reinforced buildings on the Rue du Bois.

On the southern front the 2 Brigade assault battalions, 1/Northants (Lieutenant-Colonel LGW Dobbin) and 2/Royal Sussex (Lieutenant-Colonel EBW Green), had assembled in the front line trenches, with 2/KRRC (Major LF Philips) and 1/5 Royal Sussex (Lieutenant-Colonel FG Langham), in immediate support. In reserve, beyond the

The southern attack front viewed from the German front trench line. Morning attack.

Rue du Bois, 1/9 King's Liverpool (Major TJ Bolland (who was to die in the late afternoon)) and 1/ Loyal North Lancs (Lieutenant-Colonel WD Sanderson), awaited further orders.

The lead battalions of 3 Brigade were 2/Royal Munster Fusiliers (Lieutenant-Colonel VGH Rickard, who would suffer mortal injuries) and 2/Welsh (Lieutenant-Colonel AG Prothero) with 1 /4 Royal Welch Fusiliers (Lieutenant-Colonel TC France-Hayhurst, also killed on the day) in support, and in the third line, in reserve beyond the Rue du Bois, were 1/Gloucesters (Lieutenant-Colonel AW Pagan) and 1/South Wales Borderers (Lieutenant-Colonel AJ Reddie).

After capturing and securing the German front line trenches and overwhelming the fortified positions at Ferme Cour d'Avoué and the Ferme du Bois, the battalions would regroup and hold the line along La Quinque Rue, linking with the Meerut Division to their left.

Manning the German trenches opposing 1st Division and the Meerut Division were three companies from the 1st and 3rd Battalions of the 57th Royal Prussian Regiment under the command of Hertzog Ferdinand von Braunsweig, and nine companies from the 1st and 3rd Battalions of the 55th Regiment under the command of Graf Bulow von Dennewitz.

On the right of the southern prong the bombardment was effected by 1st Division artillery – sixty-six 18-pdr guns of XXV, XXVI, XXXIX, and XLI Brigades of the RFA; twelve 15-pdr guns of V London Brigade RFA; and eighteen 13-pdr guns of N, V and X Batteries RHA detailed for wire cutting. They were lined along the Rue des Berceaux, 1400 metres distant from the enemy wire. Some 900 metres behind them, positioned to the north and south of Richebourg St Vaast, howitzers detailed to destroy the German parapets were massed.

Sixteen 6-inch guns of XII and XIV Brigades RGA; sixteen 5-inch guns of IV West Riding Brigade and VIII London Brigade and; fourteen 4.5-inch guns of XLIV Brigade RFA, were all under the direction of Brigadier-General EA Fanshawe, the 1st Divisional Artillery Commander. To their left, the combined guns of the Meerut and Lahore field artillery covered the Indian Army front.

1/ROYAL NORTH LANCS
5/ROYAL SUSSEX
2/ROYAL SUSSEX

CINDER TRACK

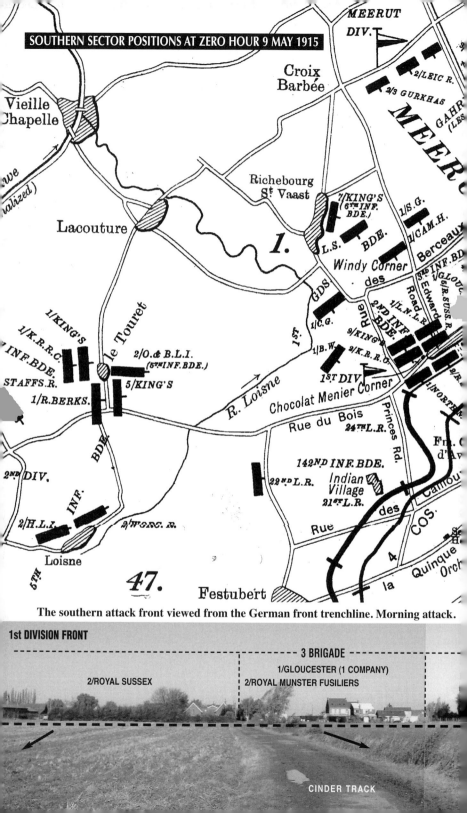

SOUTHERN SECTOR POSITIONS AT ZERO HOUR 9 MAY 1915

MEERUT DIV.

2/LEIC.R.

2/3 GURKHAS

GAHR.
(LES

MEER

Croix Barbée

Vieille Chapelle

we
ralized)

Richebourg St Vaast

7/KING'S
(6TH INF. BDE.)

1/S.G.

1/CAM.H.

Berceaux

Lacouture

1.

L.S.

BDE.

Windy Corner

des

3RD INF.BD

1/GLOU.

6/R.SUSS.R.

1/KING'S

le Touret

2/O. & B.L.I.
(5TH INF.BDE.)

GDS.

1/C.G.

Rue

1/L.N.R.

2ND INF.

Edward

1/KRRC

STAFFS.R.

1/R.BERKS.

5/KING'S

1ST

9/KING'S

1/B.W.

2/K.R.R.C.

BDE.

1/N.R.

2/R.

R. Loisne

1ST DIV.

Chocolat Menier Corner

1/NORTH

2ND DIV.

INF.

BDE.

Rue du Bois

24TH L.R.

Princes Rd.

Fn.
d'A

142ND INF.BDE.

22ND L.R.

Indian Village

21ST L.R.

Callou

COS.

2/H.L.I.

2/WORC.R.

Loisne

47.

6TH

Festubert

Rue

des

la

4

Quinque
Orch

8/
H

The southern attack front viewed from the German front trenchline. Morning attack.

1st DIVISION FRONT

- - - - - - - - - - - - - - - - - 3 BRIGADE - - - - - - - - - -

1/GLOUCESTER (1 COMPANY)
2/ROYAL MUNSTER FUSILIERS

2/ROYAL SUSSEX

CINDER TRACK

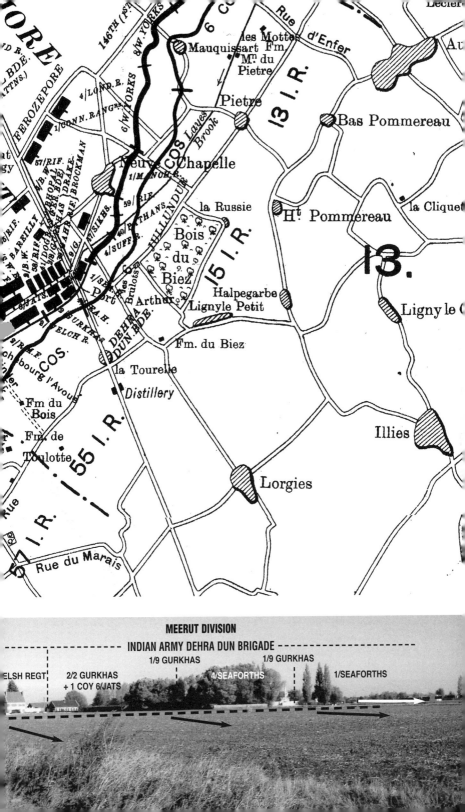

MEERUT DIVISION

- - - - - - INDIAN ARMY DEHRA DUN BRIGADE - - - - - -

| | 1/9 GURKHAS | | 1/9 GURKHAS | |
| ELSH REGT | 2/2 GURKHAS + 1 COY 6/JATS | 4/SEAFORTHS | | 1/SEAFORTHS |

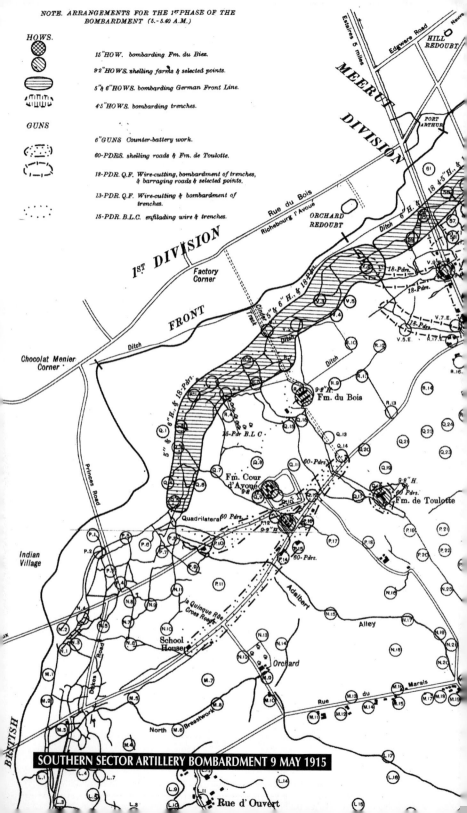

SOUTHERN SECTOR ARTILLERY BOMBARDMENT 9 MAY 1915

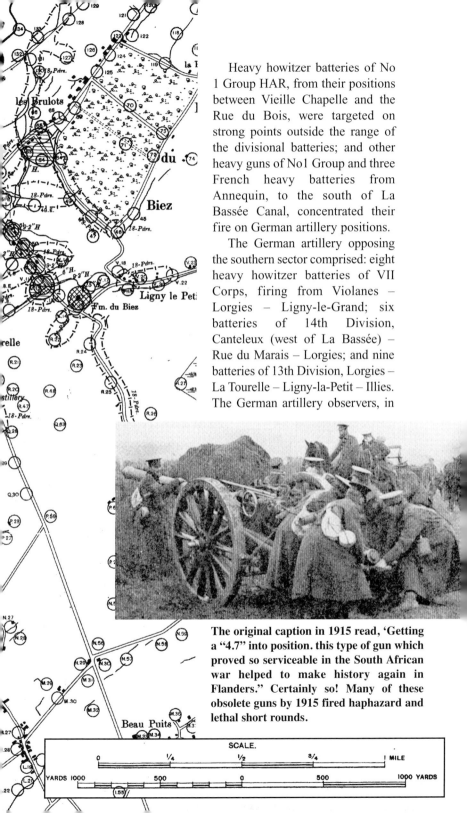

Heavy howitzer batteries of No 1 Group HAR, from their positions between Vieille Chapelle and the Rue du Bois, were targeted on strong points outside the range of the divisional batteries; and other heavy guns of No1 Group and three French heavy batteries from Annequin, to the south of La Bassée Canal, concentrated their fire on German artillery positions.

The German artillery opposing the southern sector comprised: eight heavy howitzer batteries of VII Corps, firing from Violanes – Lorgies – Ligny-le-Grand; six batteries of 14th Division, Canteleux (west of La Bassée) – Rue du Marais – Lorgies; and nine batteries of 13th Division, Lorgies – La Tourelle – Ligny-la-Petit – Illies. The German artillery observers, in

The original caption in 1915 read, 'Getting a "4.7" into position. this type of gun which proved so serviceable in the South African war helped to make history again in Flanders." Certainly so! Many of these obsolete guns by 1915 fired haphazard and lethal short rounds.

After the battle.

direct contact with their batteries from the ridge, had a perfect overview of the battlefield, the positions of the British front and reserve trench systems having long been accurately ranged and sited.

Against the northern sector the 6th Bavarian Reserve Division had twelve batteries on the ridge, Aubers – Fromelles – Le Maisnil and four heavy howitzer batteries, Herlies – Fournes.

26 Field Company Royal Engineers, based at La Couture, during April had been working with 23 Field Company in the area around Neuve Chapelle. In addition to their normal schedule, a number of extra tasks were introduced to service the forthcoming offensive. Working with parties supplied from infantry regiments, roads were repaired using broken brick from ruined houses and factories, bunkers and fortifications were constructed, pontoons built and bridges strengthened, and many unexploded shells and bombs were defused. Between 1 May and 8 May a very large number of hand grenades were made up, many used for instruction and practice, four portable bridges were constructed capable of supporting RFA heavy guns, and three similar, but lighter, for the RHA, seven moveable depots were assembled and loaded onto pontoon wagons, and two wagons were loaded with 30 feet of bridging with another 30 feet in reserve, complete with baulks and transoms. One section built a forward observation post using timbers, steel plates and sandbags to house the G.O.C. and staff, and was detailed to maintain the post during the battle.

The 1/Northants, who were to lead on the extreme right of the 1st Division attack, had been billeted in Oblingham from 3rd to 5th May cleaning kit, practising drills, and training for the assault, before moving up to Le Touret on the 6th to complete their preparations. After stacking kit and collecting the required extra battle equipment, scaling ladders, wire cutters, bridges, bombs, flags, ammunition and rations, and whilst awaiting in battle order their instructions to move forward to the designated assembly area behind the Rue de Bois, an order to stay put for 24 hours was received. 26 officers and 750 men halted to wait until the next evening.

Similarly 2/Royal Sussex, attacking to the immediate left of 1/Northants, had completed their training at Allouagne and moved to Les Falcons on 6th May, and had just started their move forward when the instruction to delay was received.

On the fine and clear Saturday evening of 8th May the two regiments started forward to assume their attack positions, a part of the vast and concerted forward movement of troops and equipment along the whole line. Captain Villiers and Captain St Croise were wounded by shell-fire whilst 2/Sussex were crossing the Rue de Bois en route to relieve the 1/Black Watch and assemble in the 400 yards wide battalion attack trenches to the right of the cinder track. Five experts from the 26 Company Royal Engineers joined their attack platoons ready to detect and defuse any booby trap mines which might have been set and primed to await the unwary in captured trenches.

To the right of the front 1/Northants settled into position. Hot tea and rum were handed out from 3.30 am and, on the stroke of 5 am, with 'noise which was terrific', the bombardment suddenly burst upon the opposing lines.

At 5.30 am, as the intensity of the shelling increased for the final ten minutes before lift, B Company lead by Captain Dickson, with D Company lead by Captain Ferrar to their left, climbed their ladders and clambered over the top of the breastworks and, using whatever cover they could find in the broken ground, under accurate spattering rifle fire, hurriedly crawled to within 150 yards of the enemy breastworks. A Company, under Captain Milne and B Company, under Captain Robinson, took their places in the trench behind the parapet ready to follow up.

2/Sussex, aligned to the left of the 1/Northants, were lead off by C and D Companies with A Company and B Company less No 8 platoon following up. No 8 platoon had been assigned to 23 (Lowland) Company RE in the Rue du Bois to carry forward sandbags and barbed wire 'to make good damage to the enemy lines' immediately after occupation. Two machine guns were sited on the battalion left flank and two more 100 yards in from the right. Battalion HQ was set up in the breastworks on the extreme right flank where 2/Sussex abutted 1/Northants. Lieutenant Austin, commanding D Company, had specified that the bombers of 14 and 16 platoons were to clear the enemy from their rear communications trenches and Sergeant Startup was to supervise the bombing of the first line trench as opportunity presented.

At 5.30 am, 9 platoon (Second Lieutenant Fewtrell), 11 platoon (Sergeant Reeves), 15 platoon (Second Lieutenant Roberts), and 16 platoon (Sergeant Wray), scrambled over the parapet and hurried forward under the barrage followed by the second line of 10 platoon (Sergeant Startup), 12 platoon (Second Lieutenant Taylor), 13 platoon (Second Lieutenant Child), and 14 platoon (Sergeant Lower). Behind them, ready to advance at 50 yard intervals in line of platoon, followed 3 platoon (Second Lieutenant Shaw) and 2 platoon (Sergeant Catchpole), then 4 platoon (Lieutenant Dicker) and 1 platoon (Second Lieutenant Talbot), then 6 platoon (Second Lieutenant Miller) and 5 platoon (Second Lieutenant Juckes).

Captain CE Bond, OC B Company, ordered 7 platoon (Second Lieutenant Wallington) to remain behind the breastworks as reserve ready to fill any gaps.

As the assault platoons emerged over the breastworks to creep into the 300 yards wide stretch of No Man's Land which lay before them, under orders to get as close as possible to the German line before the barrage lifted, the meticulously formulated tactical plan was rudely shattered by an immediate hail of bullets. Alerted by the barrage and warned by lookouts, accurate rifle fire from German infantrymen knocked many of the men back into their trenches, dead or disabled, before even surmounting their own parapets.

In spite of the obvious failure of secrecy, hurrying at the double through the bullets, many of those remaining in the assault companies of 1/Northants and 2/Royal Sussex reached midway and dropped to await the barrage lift scheduled for 5.40 am. Then, with successive waves of men likewise scrambling over the parapets behind them following in support, they ran with shouts and cheers to storm the defences ahead. As the barrage lifted the smoke became less dense and

Breastworks of hurdles and earthbags being erected by Rue du Bois during the Christmas day 'truce' 1914.

visibility improved, and the stuttering fire from the German Maxim Heavy Machine guns increased dramatically to strafe seemingly continuous fire into the hundreds of men moving towards them.

As the rapidly dwindling first lines neared the German breastworks the lack of penetration by the inadequate shellfire became horribly evident. Barbed wire remained unbroken and damage to breastworks was scant. The machine gun positions had remained undetected and were undamaged. A ditch, dug in front of the raised breastwork to facilitate the construction, had, as a final barrier, been filled with coiled barbed wire.

Captain RF Finke, commanding C Company 2/Royal Sussex on their right, was hit soon after leaving the breastworks, but carried on and was later posted missing. Second Lieutenant Taylor was wounded at the same time, but Second Lieutenant Fewtrell and his 9 platoon struggled on to within forty yards of the enemy wire, as did Captain Finch with A Company following up, although of his company officers Second Lieutenant Shaw was killed and Lieutenant Dickens and Second Lieutenant Talbot were wounded. In the leading D Company Second Lieutenant Austin was hit early and subsequently posted as missing, and Second Lieutenant Child, leading 13 platoon in the second wave, was killed. In the following B Company Second Lieutenant Muller was wounded and Lieutenant Juckes hit and his body never found. In the withering fire few managed to advance further than halfway – some got to within forty yards, and one lone soldier reached the enemy parapet before being hit and killed.

By 6.30 am the order to withdraw was issued, but many wounded, pinned down and unable to move, were forced to stay holed up in the mayhem throughout the day.

By 7.30 pm the remnants of the Battalion were marched back to billets in Les Choquaux where the roll call revealed two officers killed, nine wounded, and three missing and, of other ranks 101 dead, 118 missing, and 329 wounded.

Captain Dickson and twenty men of his B Company 1/Northants, reached a narrow breach in the defensive wire and entered the enemy trench but, according to German reports, all perished by grenade and in hand to hand fighting. All others leading the assault 'were mown down' or, were 'trapped and unable to advance or retire'.

Machine guns situated in an angle in the German front line had caused considerable casualties as massed enfilade fire was brought to bear on the exposed left flank of the advance. With all officers killed or wounded, picked off by German marksmen who recognised their putteed legs in the uniform of the day, Company Sergeant Major Butcher ordered the men to take cover and dig in. Although comments in their battalion War Diary suggest 2/Royal Musters to their left had withdrawn leaving the flank exposed, the reality was that the enemy guns were very effectively sited and concealed in the flanking salient, and although under tremendous fire, the Munsters advance had been more determined than most in striving to achieve their objectives on that fated morning.

1/5 (Cinque Ports) Battalion Royal Sussex had been holding the forward trenches fronting Richebourg L'Avoue until being relieved by the Scots Guards on 2 May and withdrawn to billets at Gonnehem. Second Lieutenant WE Price, killed by a sniper's bullet on the afternoon of 2 May whilst standing outside his dugout was, on 3 May, buried with due ceremony under the crucifix in Gonnehem churchyard. Moving to Mesplaux on 6 May the battalion moved back into the (C line) support trenches behind the Rue du Bois during the evening of 8 May, ready to attack immediately behind their regular army colleagues of 2/Royal Sussex. On their right, behind 1/Northamptonshires, was 2/KRRC and, following up in the third line of support behind them, 1/Loyal North Lancs on the left, and 9/King's (Liverpool) on the right.

1/5 Royal Sussex had started forward at 5.40 am from their reserve positions behind breastworks along the Rue du Bois under the thunderous artillery barrage. Their closely detailed orders read,

follow up immediately behind the assaulting battalions, clear all hostile trenches still occupied in the rear of both assaulting battalions and establish a strong point about Q10 (Ferme du Bois), secure all prisoners and send them to the rear, and then follow up in support. The second objectives were that A, C and D Companies continue on to secure the Ferme Cour D'Avoue and the outbuildings thereabouts. B Company was to swing right along the line of the enemy trench to move behind the KRRC to secure the flank to the left of 1/Northamptonshires.

After rapidly traversing the 200 metres of open ground between the reserve and advance trenches amidst the increasing urgency of salvos from the German field guns and redirected machine gun fire from the enemy Maxims, the men of A and C Companies 1/5 Royal Sussex desperately piled into the front trench just as the last of their comrades of 2/Sussex were scrambling to get over the top. Second Lieutenant Haig was wounded and thirty men disabled or killed during the crossing. After pausing briefly to regroup they pressed on and over the parapet to run into the same curtain of fire which had arrested the progress of 2/Sussex before them.

Behind the first broken wave of the Sussex Regiment, their second diminishing line of assault had almost reached halfway, and the third was struggling across a lateral ditch and through their own forward wire, as the fourth line emerged onto the waste of No Man's Land. Against this sea of advancing troops the German machine guns scythed back and forth without respite, the lines of men thinning and collapsing long before reaching their first objective – the German trenches. Lieutenant-Colonel Langham intervened to stop the last platoons of A and B Companies attempting to advance and was pleased to discover that Captain Courthope had issued a similar order to stop the last platoon of C Company. Lieutenant Napper was hit and

The plan of attack of 1/5 Royal Sussex Regt. extracted from War Diary. Note attack and support trenches either side of the Rue du Bois.

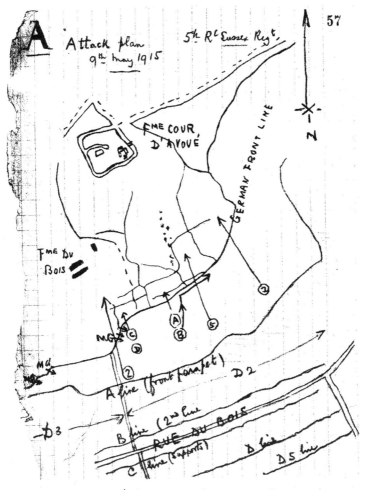

The plan of attack of 1/5 Royal Sussex Regt. extracted from War Diary. Note attack and support trenches either side of the Rue du Bois.

wounded whilst waiting in the front trench.

To add to the mayhem a German field artillery barrage, concentrated on the crowded No Man's Land and the British front and reserve trenches sustained a relentless rate of fire.

Captain Ferris Nelson Grant MC, the much-respected commander of B Company, 1/5 Sussex, an ex-Royal Navy officer who had for some time served as a private soldier before being eventually persuaded to apply for commission, roused those around him by standing and waving the red company marker flag, urging and shouting to his men to move to their right to link up with 1/Northants. He was shot dead and only a handful of his troops survived.

At about 7 am the orders to retire were received. Sergeant Roberts crossed on three separate occasions to the firing line, under extreme fire, to convey orders to withdraw. The battalion was to regroup in reserve trenches (D5) behind the Rue du Bois in readiness for another assault in the afternoon.

Roll call revealed that Captains FN Grant and TA Stewart-Jones, and Second Lieutenants REM Dennison, RE Powell and R Fazan were dead, and Major EH Langham, and Second Lieutenants Dodd, Perry and Hobart wounded. 230 other ranks were posted as killed wounded or missing.

At about 2 pm the battalion moved forward again to support the afternoon assault behind 1/Black Watch. The lead battalions failed in that futile but heroic repeat and, at 6 pm, those remaining of 1/5 Sussex reformed in a field behind Chocolat Menier Corner then marched back via Le Touret to Gonnehem. There they rested for a day, before again marching on to billets in the Tobacco Factory on the Rue de Lille in Bethune.

2/King's Royal Rifle Corps, following up in support of the 1/Northants, were detailed to capture and fortify the German trench line which ran at right angles to the main front towards la Quinque Rue. 'At all costs' they were there to hold a defensive line 800 yards long to secure the right flank of the whole attack. Arriving at Essars at 6pm on the 6 May 'after an uncomfortable march on the hot and sunny day', they started forward at 7.25 pm on 8 May, having stored packs the previous day and, delayed by 24 hours, were finally assembled in the support trenches by 2 am on 9 May.

With A Company on the right and C Company on the left leading, followed by B Company and D Company in the same order in support, the lead platoons started over the support trench parapets at 5.25 am as the Northants in front of them attacked and, without pause, poured into and over the front parapet to be instantly ripped by the inferno of fire and 'very heavy shelling'. The leading platoons 'came to within 30 yards of the German wire having rushed forward with great dash', before the last man fell. Captain Harris was seriously wounded and Second Lieutenant Farmer took over command of C Company. Those capable were ordered to withdraw and regroup in the support trenches. The remains of B and D Companies were sent forward again to hold the front line trench whilst the 1st Division attacked during the afternoon, and returned at 6.30 pm to join the survivors of A and C Companies behind the Rue du Bois. The stretcher-bearers under Second Lieutenant Collins searched throughout the hours of darkness and recovered twenty eight wounded. Just after midnight the remaining bedraggled riflemen started their march back to billets in Essars.

Lieutenant WW McBride and Second Lieutenant JI Farmer were missing, and Captain EMJ Upton, Lieutenant W Hodges, Lieutenant WS Bird, and Second Lieutenant CW Morris had been killed. Of other ranks 80 were posted as missing, forty two were killed, and 118 wounded.

2 Brigade attack had been totally arrested.

Across the width of the front, ragged and dismembered groups were pinned down frantically seeking whatever scant shelter they could in craters and ditches, in the torn earth, and amongst the wreckage of battle. Surrounded by dead and dying men amidst the acrid smells and

smoke, all were bathed in the warm sunshine of that fatal Sunday morning.

The 1/Northants War Diary records that, due to the concentration of the opposing fire, 'it was impossible to gain position' and within thirty minutes 'the assault had obviously failed'. Hundreds of trapped and wounded men lay out in the bullet and shell torn No Man's Land until the darkness of the night afforded cover to crawl and drag themselves back to their lines, many having been isolated for over fourteen hours. Medics and stretcher-bearers repeated heroic journeys time and time again under the cover of darkness into the churned up mess to recover wounded. Special mention is made of Lieutenant Bordillon, the Medical Officer, who 'worked on without respite and carried out invaluable work on the recovered'.

Those 1/Northants remaining assembled at Le Touret from where they marched back to billets at Oblingham, arriving at 9.30 pm on 10 May.

1/Northants diary records: eight officers killed and nine wounded, and 541 other ranks killed, missing, and wounded.

The dead officers were Second in Command Major WO Cantley DSO; B Company Captain BB Dickson, Second Lieutenant R Davison, Second Lieutenant H Thompson; C Company Lieutenant RS Cowley; D Company Captain JH Farrar, Captain TG Powell, and Second Lieutenant KE Munro.

Wounded were: A Company, Captain EC Mylne, and Second Lieutenant Attwater; B Company, Second Lieutenant RS Champion, and Lieutenant TC Fulton; C Company, Second Lieutenant HH Forbes, Lieutenant Nye, Second Lieutenant Norman, and Second Lieutenant V Clark.

1/Loyal North Lancs Regiment, as a reserve battalion, had been ordered to press ahead in support of the attack along the sector fronted by 1/Northants, 2/Sussex, and 1/5 Sussex. Their training had been very thorough, but would prove to be of no avail against the impenetrable shield of defensive fire through which they were also ordered to advance.

On 7 May bivouaced at Les Casan, the battalion had practised anti-gas techniques, field drills, and rehearsed the forthcoming assembly and assault repeatedly. All ranks were issued with 220 rounds of ammunition, gas mask, two sandbags, and a groundsheet. Each assault platoon collected red flags which were fastened on nine foot long poles, to be used to signal the position of the advance firing line back to the artillery batteries, and white sheets to signal positions to the spotter planes above. Packs were dumped at Maisplaix Farm and additional assault equipment – picks, shovels, bridges, scaling ladders, and extra hand bombs – were issued. The 5 pm entry in the Battalion War Diary states 'The men are in splendid spirits and all ready. Everything promises well'. The battalion was all set to march forward at the appointed time of 8.30 pm. The order postponing the action was received at about 7 pm and it instead moved to billets in Les Choquaux. On 8 May the arrival of Second Lieutenant F Holmes and Second Lieutenant G Hawkesley, seconded from the 4/Royal Inskilling Fusiliers, brought the battalion up to a fighting strength of 19 officers and 806 men. At 8 pm the move up to reserve positions behind the Rue du Bois started. At 4 am 'a beautiful morning with a gentle breeze from the north west' is recorded and, at 5.30 am, surrounded by the thunder of artillery and with shells screeching overhead, A and B Companies, followed by C and D Companies, crossed the Rue du Bois to begin their thirty minute journey to the front reserve trenches.

On arrival the failure of the first step was evident. Although the bombardment had been terrific the enemy wire was not properly cut and men of 2/Sussex and 1/Northants with some 5/Sussex were lying in the open only 100 yards from the enemy wire.

At 6.45 am, ordered to assault, A, B, and D Companies pushed and struggled through the congestion behind the breastworks and just before 7 am were struggling over the parapet.

The enemy fire was terrible. Many machine guns on our left flank. Before 100 yards had been covered the whole line was checked. Some managed to get back.

At 7.45 am orders were issued to withdraw under cover of a short bombardment aimed at the German breastworks. On withdrawal the battalion was ordered to hold the front line at all costs alongside 9/King's (Liverpool). The battalion witnessed the attack by the 1st Division at 4pm, '1/Black Watch attacked magnificently' and, having been shelled constantly throughout the day, was relieved by 2/Highland Light Infantry (2nd Division) at about 3 am on 10 May.

The survivors of 1/Loyal North Lancs marched back via Le Touret to billets at Long Cornet. Only one officer per company had survived, including the signals officer, Lieutenant Diver, officially attached to HQ. Captain GW Hay, Captain SJ Adcock, Lieutenant R Potter, and Lieutenant TW Williams, were dead. Second Lieutenant W Fisher, Second Lieutenant F Holmes, Second Lieutenant TM Garrod, Captain Hill (who was brought in during the following night), and Lieutenant Fisher, the machine gun officer, who was struck in the head later in the day, all died of wounds at Bethune Hospital, and Second Lieutenant Roy, Second Lieutenant Scott, Second Lieutenant Waterworth, and Second Lieutenant Morris were wounded. Casualties amongst other ranks totalled nineteen killed, 190 wounded and twenty-one were posted as missing.

To the left of 2 Brigade the lead battalions of 3 Brigade, 2/Royal Munster Fusiliers and 2/Welsh, faced a similar torrent of fire as they emerged.

2/Royal Munster Fusiliers had been based at La Jomoe Willot from 3 to 7 May, training, route marching and, according to their War Diary, particularly 'practising leaving trenches and assaulting'. Their march to the front started at 7.15 pm on 8 May and, after 'Father Gleeson gave absolutions at the first halt on the road', they arrived without mishap at about midnight to relieve 1/Coldstream Guards in the forward trenches. The battalion was positioned on the right of 3 Brigade front, their right flank abutting the cinder track, and their left some 300 yards from that track at the ditch separating the battalion from 2/Welsh. They in turn covered the remainder of the brigade front as far as the west edge of Orchard Redoubt. Behind the two assault battalions 1/4 R Welsh Fusiliers moved into second line trenches ready to fill the assault trenches as soon they were vacated to then go over the top to back up the 5.40 am attack.

Ordered over the top at 5.35 am, and under constant fire from the moment they appeared over the parapets, B Company, 2/Munsters on the right rushed to within ninety yards of the German breastworks. The two lead platoons of A Company to their left scrambled along a system of disused and damaged trenches for a further thirty yards. There they paused to await the barrage lift, then, with C and D Companies following immediately, rushed forward. Despite increasing numbers falling dead or wounded, about one hundred of B Company managed to reach the breastworks, although others were pinned down and trapped by the now ferocious machine gun fire and desperate salvos of rifle bullets.

The guarding wire works had, for a short stretch, been severely mauled by the British artillery, and the third platoon of 11/55 Regiment in the trench immediately ahead had nearly all been wiped out.

Captain Campbell-Dick had been shot dead whilst standing atop the parapet waving his hat and urging men over. Lieutenant-Colonel Rickard, commanding 2/Munsters, who lead his men with great determination through deadly crossfire, was hit and mortally wounded and fifty others were killed whilst forcing their way through the tangled jumble of barbed wire and posts. The fifty remaining crossed the barbed wire filled ditch and over the parapet to occupy the German front trench, then again, in a forward rush, overran the second line trench, surprising and trapping most of the men of the 11/55 Regiment remaining there.

However, the scant success was short lived and retribution was swift. Lead by Oberleutnant Herbert Reuter, the bombers of the 55th Regiment attacked the men of 2/Munsters down the first line trench from the flanks, overpowering and killing all but eight therein, who were taken prisoner. Those who had pressed forward were assailed by rifle fire from their rear as German infantrymen wrested possession of the second line trench over which they had stormed and, using the parados as firestep, isolated the dwindling party. A deep ditch filled with muddy water trapped the few remaining Munsters. Some who tried to struggle across became entangled in barbed wire laid below the surface and drowned, and the few still remaining gallantly dug in along the bank and somehow held out until blown to pieces by British shells when the bombardment preceding the afternoon attack burst upon them. Three survived the ordeal to become prisoners of war.

Instances of great heroism on both sides abounded during this brief spell of intense combat. Private Ziegenbein, the 11/55 Company bugler who had, whilst closely protecting his commanding officer, shot a number of threatening Munsters, on being hit himself collapsed against his Commanding Officer and before dying pointed to the rear saying, 'Sir! The English! Behind us!' Weinberg, the German war artist, depicts the scene in his painting, *The 11/55 in the Battle of May 1915 near La Bassée.*

The most destructive fire – concentrated rifles. Here firing through slots built into the breastworks.

At 6.15 am 1/South Wales Borderers and 1/Gloucesters moved forward toward the front line trench, Major Graham took command over the depleted 2/Munsters, and those remaining capable, and the four battalion machine guns were ordered to withdraw to the reserve trenches. At 10.30 am just over 200 men and four remaining officers withdrew to the rear of the Rue du Bois. There they reformed in readiness for a renewed attack in the afternoon, A and B Companies under Second Lieutenant Carrigan, and C and D Companies under Lieutenant Keating and Second Lieutenant Harcourt, whilst Sergeant Gannion was detailed to take charge of the machine gunners.

Brigadier General Davies told me personally twice during the day that he considered the Regiment had behaved very gallantly and had done all that could be done.

The War Diary of 2/Munsters further records that

3.20 to 4 pm : sharp rifle fire was maintained by the Germans in spite of the bombardment on their lines.

4.05 pm : Forward movement into 1st Trench stopped by impasse as Gloucesters stopped by heavy fire.

At 7 pm the battalion formed up behind the Rue du Bois and marched back to billets at La Jomoe Willot, arriving at 10.30pm on 9 May. Roll call revealed six officers killed, six missing, and seven wounded, and other ranks suffered fifty killed, 129 missing, and 191 wounded.

Lieutenant Colonel VGH Rickard, the commanding officer, is buried in Cabaret-Rouge cemetery, Souchez.

An addendum to the Battalion War Diary records a message relayed from GOC 3 Brigade to C.O. 2/Royal Munster Fusiliers.

I wish you to convey to the officers of 2/RMF my appreciation of the fine example set to the Division by the successful assault of part of his leading line: a feat of arms which the Battalion must always be proud of, as the Battalion was the only one in the Brigade whose men succeeded in storming the enemy breastworks.

Sgd : R Haking Major-General Commanding 1st Division.

1st Div. HQ 11 May 1915.

Abutting 2/Munsters on their left, 2/Welsh, although closer to the German lines – the No Man's Land before them was about a hundred metres wide – had three water filled ditches barring their crossing and faced a great intensity of head on fire.

At 5.30 pm on 7 May the battalion had paraded and left their billets at Le Cornet, only to be intercepted outside Locon by a motor cycle orderly bearing orders to delay the move for twenty four hours – the whole battalion about turned and marched back to Le Cornet. At 5.30 pm on 8 May the march forward was repeated, arriving in assembly trenches behind the Rue du Bois to the left side of 2/Munsters with whom they shared the 750 yard wide brigade attack front. They moved forward to the attack trenches with C Company under Captain WM Howe on the right, and B Company under Captain TP Aldworth on the left, followed immediately behind by D Company under Captain H Farker, and A Company under Captain MM Campbell. Timed at 5.37 am, the two lead platoons of each company hurried over the parapets, followed by the support platoons three minutes later. As the last of the soldiers cleared the parapet and the barrage lifted, the War Diary records, 'such an increase in machine gun and accurate heavy rifle fire as to make advance impossible'.

From the eleven lead officers, eight were immediately killed or disabled. A Company recorded three officers and seventy six men becoming casualties before even accessing the front trench. Trapped by heavy and sustained fire in the churned up muddy mess fronting their lines, even those remaining capable were unable to get back until the early afternoon, when a short bombardment provided some respite.

Roll call revealed that Lieutenants FTP Wells, HGA Corder, JTC Vincent, and GRM Crofts, and Second Lieutenants JW Betts and HC Woodroffe, had been killed :

Captain MIM Campbell, Captain TP Aldworth, Captain WM Howe, and Lieutenant L Margrave were wounded, and of the other ranks fifty nine were dead, 154 wounded, and thirty two were missing.

After a long wait in forward reserve anticipating further action as part of the afternoon attempt, the tattered battalion under the command of Captain AG Lyttleton, starting off at 7 pm, moved back the eight miles to Pont Hinges,.

Second Lieutenant BUS Cripps, 2/Welsh, in a letter dated a week after the attack, describes his experience:

> *We were told that after the bombardment there would not be many people left in the German first and second lines. We were all quite confident of the result and were very cheery. I got about two hours sleep and then had breakfast and plenty of rum and felt quite ready for any German. My platoon was not to leave the trench for two minutes after the first two platoons had gone. At 5.37 am the first two platoons jumped over the parapet ready to charge but they were met by a perfect hail of bullets and many men just fell back into the trench riddled with bullets. A few survivors managed to get into one of the ditches. My company*

commander then turned to me before my two minutes were up and said I had better try. So I took my platoon and the other platoon in the company also came and we jumped up over the parapet to charge but we met with the same fate and I with a few men managed to get into the ditch. I was the only officer left in my company, two being killed outright and my company commander and another subaltern severely wounded. So I had to take command of my company. I had fifteen unwounded men with me, and heaps of wounded and dead. There was no means of getting back to the trench except by walking along the ditch for about fifty yards in water and mud up to your middle. This method was of course impossible as we had so many wounded. So after we had bound up the wounded as best we could we started to dig our way back. The Germans were firing as hard as they could at first with their heads and shoulders looking over their parapet and there were any amount of them. It took us about three hours to get the trench dug and another hour to move the wounded, All the time we were out there the Germans dropped shells all around us and our own guns dropped a lot amongst us. I was covered with earth once but was not hurt, I had a bullet through my hat and through my hair but it did not draw blood. I was soaked up to my waist and had to sit with dead and dying all around me. It was absolutely past words, my best friends killed and we could do nothing about it.

A soldier drags a body out of the mire.

From 5 May 1/Gloucesters, billeted around Les Choquaux and Long Cornet, had been training intensively for the assault, spending time on manoeuvres and practising close fighting techniques in the Bois de Pacault. On 5 May the commanding officer, Major GF Gardiner, reported ill, and Captain AW Pagan assumed command. He and his company commanders reconnoitred the battleground on 6 May before returning in the evening to attend a regimental concert at Locon. On 7 May a move to new billets in Tannoy was completed at midnight. After a rest and a change to battle order the battalion marched forward on the evening of 8 May to arrive at Windy Corner at 11.30 pm, then on to occupy the fourth line reserve trenches behind the Rue du Bois, positioned to the right of 1/South Wales Borderers. Bombs, ammunition, rations and respirators were drawn during the night in readiness for the morning attack.

With C Company on the right of the leading line and B Company on the left, D Company formed up behind them in support. A Company had been attached to 23 Field Company RE. The 3rd Division attack orders detailed that the battalion was to move through the assault battalions and to press the advance to secure the line from Ferme du Bois to the Distillerie. Ordered forward at 5.40 am as the assault battalions scrambled over the parapets after the opening bombardment, C and B Companies pushed into the chaos mounting in the front lines to assume their positions in the assault and support trenches, under orders to press their attack at 7 am after a further short but intense local bombardment. Unable to form properly,

due to the many of other corps [sic] *who were crowding the trenches, the lead platoons scrambled over the top in ragged order under very intense machine gun fire which had resumed immediately after the bombardment.*

Bogged down forty yards in front of the parapets C Company reported the loss of 2 officers and 60 men before being ordered to withdraw and to regroup in the third line trench behind the Rue du Bois alongside the 1/South Wales Borderers.

On 8 May, having marched on 7th from billets in Hingette to Les Chocques only to be ordered to return, 1/South Wales Borderers again marched, passing through Locon at 8 pm, to arrive at Windy Corner at 10 pm, and on to assemble in the third line trenches on the west side of the Rue du Bois in Brigade reserve. With C Company on the right and D Company on the left and, in the fourth line, A Company behind C, and B Company behind D, they waited the move forward at zero hour. At 5.40 am, as the lead battalions attacked, the battalion struggled to assume positions in the front and second line trenches, ready to follow up behind the 2/Welsh and 2/R Munsters, but, due to the chaos as the opening assault ahead of them disintegrated, and pushing in vain against a confusion of troops repelled by enemy fire and maimed and wounded milling around, the battalion backed out to again regroup in the second and third line trenches. Lieutenants MV Pollock and the Rt. Hon. GP French were killed by enemy fire during the aborted manoeuvre. Here, continually bombarded, the battalion awaited further orders.

On the 1st Division front, the Brigade Commanders, Davies (3rd) and Thesiger (2nd) both asked Major-General Haking, commanding the Division, for further artillery bombardments and, after some deliberation, a further bombardment was ordered to precede a renewed attack ordered for 7 am. Lieutenant-General Anderson agreed to support the attack with another attempt by the Dehra Dun Brigade.

The forward areas were crammed with dead, dying and wounded, and the many hundreds more lying out in No Man's Land were sprayed with erratically scattered shrapnel under the faulty bombardment. Although German infantrymen in the fire trenches suffered, the well-sheltered machine gun posts were virtually untouched.

The hopelessness of effectively marshalling a renewed attack at such short notice was obvious to all at the front, but unfortunately not to those directing the battle from divisional headquarters in the rear.

On the 2 Brigade front men of the 2/Royal Sussex and 1/5 Royal Sussex, ordered back to their lines, many supporting injured comrades, found themselves struggling against three companies of 1/Loyal North Lancashire Regt, the reserve battalion, which had been ordered forward at the double only to run into the same constant fire. The 1/Loyals lost thirteen officers and 250 men in quick time. The enemy wire barrier still remained hardly cut and, with rare exceptions, impenetrable.

On the 3 Brigade front, the remains of those battalions already repulsed in the first attack were regrouped and the attempts to attack repeated.

The battle plan was that 1/South Wales Borderers and 1/Gloucesters would sweep through the lead battalions to secure the second objectives but, with forward movement stagnated, their involvement in the morning action was rendered marginal and ineffective. Both battalions were ordered to wait in forward lines ready to lead an afternoon offensive. They remained on full alert under constant bombardment, surveying the broken ground of No Man's Land across which they would soon have to attack. The groans and cries of those isolated and wounded assailed their senses amidst the explosions, billowing smoke and sprays of mud continually drenching them.

At 7.20 am. Major-General Haking, commanding 1st Division, advised Lieutenant-General Monro, his Corps Commander, that the second attack was, like the first, a failure. On requesting permission to commit his reserve Guards Brigade, he was curtly told to do nothing before being specifically instructed to do so.

B. DAWN Attack – Indian CORPS (from the Rue du Bois).
On the southern front, to the left of the 1st Division, the Dehra Dun Brigade, under the command of Brigadier-General CW Jacob, awaited in the frontline trenches with orders to attack and capture the 800 yards wide stretch of German trenches fronting them. These orders state they were then to secure further specific objectives beyond: the small group of houses known as La Tourelle; the Distillery; the recently fortified Ferme du Biez; the villages of Ligny-le Petit and Ligny-le-Grand; and then capture and secure the strong point at La Cliqueterie Farm.

OPERATIONAL ORDER NO 21.
by
Brigadier-General C.W.JACOB.
Commanding Dehra Dun Brigade 6th May 1915

Reference map of Assembly forwarded under my No B.M. 22 of 5 May.
1. The Brigade will move into position of Assembly by 11 p.m. on May 7th preparatory to attack at dawn.
2. All movements will be via St VAAST Corner M.32 d – track alongside Trolley line – past LANSDOWNE POST to RUE DU BOIS. The only communication trench to be used between LANSDOWNE POST and RUE DU BOIS is that known as ORCHARD Communication trench.
3. The 1st Seaforths will pass ST VAAST POST, by Companies at 10 minutes interval, commencing at 8 p.m. and will enter the Assembly area from the RUE DU BOIS by the three first Communication trenches crossing the RUE DU BOIS west of PORT ARTHUR cross roads i.e. PIONEER Communication Trench – CRESCENT Communication trench and the trench leading to the centre of CRESCENT trench.
4. The 2nd Gurkhas will leave FORESTERS LANE by Companies at 10 minutes interval commencing at 8 p.m. Companies marching from billets not to pass ST VAAST POST before 8.30 p.m. and will enter the Assembly area by the Communication trenches leading into and through the ORCHARD.
5. The 4th Seaforths will pass ST VAAST POST by Companies at 10 minutes interval, commencing at 9 p.m. and will enter the Assembly area by the two Communication trenches leading into centre of CRESCENT Trench and the new trench near West end

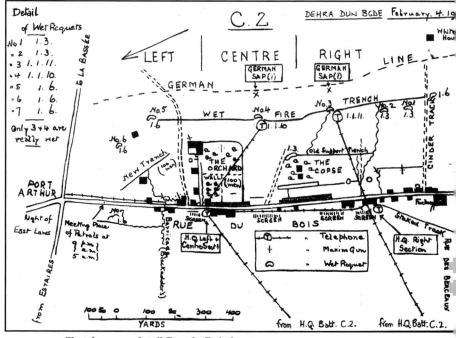

Sketch map – detail Rue du Bois front.

of CRESCENT Trench.

6. The 9th Gurkhas will pass ST VAAST POST by Companies at 10 minutes interval commencing at 9.40 p.m. and will enter the assembly area by the same communication trenches as the 1st Seaforths.

7. The 6th Jats will pass ST VAAST POST in two parties at 10.20 p.m. 10.30 p.m. and will enter the Assembly area via the Communication trenches leading from RUE DU BOIS towards North end of ORCHARD.

8. Ladders and Bridges will be carried up by companies.

9. The importance of absence of noise both during the march and when in the Assembly area is to be impressed on all ranks. Also the vital necessity of men keeping hidden from view as much as possible after dawn while the Artillery is registering and cutting wire.

10. Brigade Report Centre will be established at '96 Picadilly' after 8.30 p.m. on May the 7th.

Issued at 7 p.m. Sg   H.A.WALKER
Major Bde Major Dehra Dun Brigade.

68

OPERATION ORDER NO 32.
by
Brigadier-General C.W. JACOB.
Commanding Dehra Dun Brigade. 7th May 1915.

Information.

1 (a). The 1st Army is attacking on May the 8th.

(b) The 1st Corps retaining right on GIVENCHY is to advance RUE DU MARAIS   LORGIES   and ILLIES.

(c). The Indian Corps is to operate so as to cover the left of the 1st Corps capturing the FERME DU BIEZ and advancing on line LIGNY- LE- GRAND – LA CLIQUETERIE FERME.

(d). The 4th Corps is to turn the AUBERS Defences by an attack from North East and subsequently to gain touch with the Indian Corps at LA CLIQUETERIE FERME.

(e). The Meerut Division is to make the attack to be delivered by the Indian Corps.

(f). The Lahore Division is to hold the front allotted to the Indian Corps less that portion from which the Meerut Division is to attack. It will assist the left flank of the Meerut attack by fire. It will also open a communication trench from the Listening Post at Point 61 to connect up with the attack if this becomes desirable.

Intention.

2. The Dehra Dun Brigade will break the enemy's line from Point V.6. to 56 and establish itself on the front Distillery (Square S.17.a.c.) – FERME DU BIEZ – Point 53.

Orders to Troops.

3.(a). The 2nd Gurkhas will break the enemy's line between Point V.6. and the ditch which runs at right angles to the German trenches about Point 58. Subsequently working in conjunction with the right of the 4th Seaforths. The Battalion will push on towards the line R.16.E – LE TOURELLE cross roads. The Left Flank should reach the ESTAIRES – La Bassée Road near Point V.9.E. whence it should push up the road clearing the houses on the West side.

The Battalion will establish itself on the above line but if circumstances permit will push forward a detachment to seize and occupy the DISTILLERY.

(b). The 4th Seaforths will break the enemy's line from east of ditch mentioned in (a) and the La Bassée Road. Subsequently working in conjunction with the left of the 2nd Gurkhas, the Battalion will push on to the line LE TOURELLE Cross road – Point V.8. and the right flank should clear the houses on the East side of the road.

(c). The 1st Seaforths will break the enemy's line between the LA BASSEE Road and Point 56. Subsequently the Battalion will push on towards Point V.8. and road junction immediately east of V.12. A protective flank is to be established facing the BOIS DU BIEZ along the road leading from Point 53 to V.12. The Battalion will establish itself in the above line, but if circumstances permit will push forward a detachment to seize and occupy the FERME DU BIEZ.

(d). The 6th Jats will support the 2nd Gurkhas and as soon as the latter Battalion has reached its objective will push forward and occupy the DISTILLERY. It will move forward to the trenches vacated by the 2nd Gurkhas as soon as the latter advance to the assault.

(e). Two Companies 9th Gurkhas will support the 1st Seaforths and as soon as the latter Battalion has gained its object will push forward and occupy the FERME DU BIEZ. They will move forward to the trenches W of La Bassée Road vacated by 1st Seaforths as soon as the latter Battalion advance to the assault. 9th Gurkas (less 2 Coys) will act as Brigade Reserve and will occupy the front line of trenches vacated by 4th Seaforths as soon the latter move forward, sending a British Officer to Brigade Head Quarters to await any instructions.

(f). During night 7th / 8th May   Officers Commanding Assaulting Battalions will arrange to cut the wire in their front to allow of exit and will place bridges in position as far as possible. Every effort should be made to conceal the Bridges.
This work should be done before the moon rises at 2.07 a.m.

(g). The 3 Assaulting Battalions will form up in front of our advanced trenches after the wire cutting portion of the bombardment is completed at 5.20 a.m. and before the bombardment of the enemy's trenches ends at 5.40 a.m. The assaulting line will, during the bombardment, move up as close to the enemy's line as our shell fire permits, and will reach the enemy's front line trenches at the earliest possible moment after this bombardment is lifted to more distant objectives at 5.40 a.m.

(h). The following points as captured will be held by garrisons and strengthened. Parties of Sappers and Pioneers will be sent under orders of C.R.E. to assist :-

(a). South end of LE TOURELLE Village.

(b). Distillery.

(c). Road junction in S.11.a (Points 52 and 53).

(d). Group of houses near Point 50.

(e). FERME DU BIEZ.

Ammunition

4.(a) Men will carry 200 rounds on the person.

(b).Part of the Regimental Reserve S.A.A. should be collected at convenient places in the forward line trenches and Units should endeavour to have these carried forward behind the attack and to establish a forward Depot. This can be done either by detailing the rear Company to carry forward a certain number of boxes or by leaving parties from each Company with orders to follow some distance behind or when they see the Distinguishing flags hoisted in certain localities.

(c). A Depot of S.A.A. has been established in the RUE DU BOIS near the R.E. Depot shown on the Assembly map. All Officers and N.C.O.'s should know where this is.

(d). The two supporting Battalions, 9th Gurkhas and 6th Jats, will arrange to carry forward additional boxes of ammunition to some forward locality.

(e). Depots of ammunition have been or will be established as shown on Assembly map at Head of Communication trenches and also in the Listening Post East of PORT ARTHUR.

Grenades and Bombs

5. A Reserve of Grenades and Bombs has been collected in dug outs as shown on the Assembly map, and all concerned should know the locality.

Sandbags

6. Every man will carry two sandbags.

Distinguishing Flags

7. (a).Flags 3 ft x 3 ft – Red and black divided diagonally and with a white diagonal cross have been issued and should be stuck up on the reverse side of prominent points gained to mark the progress of the attack.

(b).Troops of the 8th Division will show a Red Flag 2ft 6in. square with a white or yellow diagonal stripe. Blocking parties of Bombers will show a red flag 1ft 3in. square.

(c).Troops of the 7th Division will show a flag 3 ft. long by 2 ft. Broad with three horizontal stripes two red and one white.

(d).Troops of the 1st Division will show a red flag with white vertical stripe in centre.

(e). Lahore Division will show a yellow flag.

Masks 8.
Masks will be kept in readiness soaked in the solution, by all troops in the front trenches and will be worn by assaulting troops.

No. 4 Trench Battery R.A. and Bomb Guns.
9. No.4 Trench Battery R.A. after the Artillery has cut wire and while the bombardment of trenches is going on will fire on V.8. Brigade Bomb Gun Officer will detail two guns to proceed with each assaulting Battalion. These will be used to bomb localities which hold out obstinately.

Signals 10. Each unit will carry two helios in addition to other Signal Equipment.

Medical 11. A collecting Station will be established between LANSDOWNE POST and the Tramway where it crosses FORESTERS LANE. Route for the wounded returning from the front will be by the ORCHARD Communication trench which runs from RUE DU BOIS to FORESTERS LANE along the North East side of the Tramway.

Prisoners 12. Prisoners will be handed over to Lahore Division at Dehra Dun Report Centre.

Official time.
13. Official time will be given to Units at Brigade Head Quarters after 6 p.m. on May the 7th – two watches to be sent by each representative.

Reports 14. RUE DU BOIS near Communication trench leading into ORCHARD.

> Issued at 9 a.m. Sgd H.A. Walker Major.
> Brigade Major Dehra Dun Brigade.

The assault battalions of the Dehra Dun Brigade were, on the right, 2/2 Gurkhas (Colonel ERP Boileau) with a company of the 6/Jats attached; holding the centre ground, 1/4 Seaforth Highlanders

72

(Lieutenant-Colonel TW Cuthbert) and, on their left, stretching north-east from the Estaires – La Bassée road towards Neuve Chapelle, 1/Seaforth Highlanders (Lieutenant-Colonel AB Richie).

As the front line trenches were vacated by the Dehra Dun brigade, a two battalions strong special force from the Garhwal brigade, 39/Garhwalis and 2/8 Gurkhas, were to occupy positions on the left front ready to move forward to attack and secure, concurrently with the main brigade assault on Ligny-le-Petit, the eastern edge of the Bois du Biez and then to capture and occupy the strong point of la Russie off the north east corner of the wood.

The Bareilly Brigade waited in reserve trenches behind the Rue du Bois in immediate support of the Dehra Dun Brigade, and the Garhwal Brigade, less the two battalions forming the special force, were held in divisional reserve.

The artillery of the Meerut and Lahore Divisions, under the command of Brigadier-General FE Johnson, combined to provide the opening bombardment, with additional support by guns of the No1 Group Heavy Artillery Reserve, commanded by Brigadier-General G McK Franks. The 18-pdr guns of the Meerut Division, from a range of 1800 metres, were detailed to clear barbed wire, whilst three RFA brigades of the Lahore Division from positions west of Neuve

Seaforths filling their water-bottles at a town pump before going into the trenches.

Indian artillery en route to the front.

Chapelle were to barrage the sector north of the Lorgies road to hinder German troop movement. Eighteen 4.5 inch howitzers of XLIII Brigade RFA; and eight 6 inch howitzers of VI Brigade RGA were detailed to destroy the 700 metres of German parapet opposite.

No. 1 Group H.A.R., assembled between Vieille Chapelle and the Rue du Bois, consisted of 1 x 15 inch howitzer of the RMA; 4 x 9.2 inch howitzers 10th Siege Battery; 2 x 9.2 inch howitzers 13th Siege Battery; 4 x 60 pdrs 24th Heavy Battery; 4 x 60 pdrs 48th Heavy Battery; and 4 x 60 pdrs of 1st Canadian Heavy Battery. All were detailed to destroy specific fortified strong points and German batteries between Violaines and Ligny le Grand, beyond the range of the divisional artilleries. Additional firepower from three French heavy artillery batteries near Annequin, south of the La Bassée canal, was detailed to disable German batteries between the La Bassée canal and Violaines. Although aerial reconnaissance in the weeks preceding the battle had approximated the positions of German batteries, movement was frequent and the low flat terrain and the many pollarded willows in full leaf prevented efficient detection of enemy gun positions by forward artillery observation officers on the ground. The twenty-three opposing German batteries, including eight heavy batteries, were well sited and perfectly ranged on the lines from which the Indian Division assaults were to be launched.

The bombardment, which started at 5.00 am, focused on the German front lines, from 5.30 am became intense, the shrapnel firing guns working on wire-cutting, then switching to HE to inflict as much destruction as possible on the opposing breastworks.

The barbed wire in front of the German line was reported as being satisfactorily cut before the guns lifted. However, casualties due to short falling shells were reported from the 2/2Gurkhas and the Seaforth Highlanders positions, and alarm was registered in both battalion war diaries regarding the lack of visible damage to the German breastworks. At 5.40 am the guns lifted some 600 yards to the line of La Quinque Rue and concentrated fire on specific forward positions - until 6 am the strongpoint of La Tourelle, then the Distillery fortifications until 6.30 am.

Starting at 5.25 am under cover of the barrage, 1/Seaforths and 1/4 Seaforths climbed slowly over and down in front of their breastworks and formed up with the intention of moving stealthily across the narrow stretch of No Man's Land to within a few yards of the enemy. Short falling shells exploding in their midst frustrated the carefully laid plan and prevented advance and, instead, they were forced to crouch in front of their own parapets to await the barrage lift at 5.40 am.

On the right front of the Indian Brigade parapet was a water-filled ditch four to five yards wide across which many footbridges had been carefully laid during the preceding night. Parapet ladders were placed in readiness for quick exits at zero hour, and exit paths had been cut through the guarding wire during the preceding hours of darkness to ensure the advance of the attackers would be unhindered.

Just before the deafening mayhem of the opening barrage increased to its climactic final ten minutes, the two platoons of 6/Jats and Nos 2

The La Bassée – Estaires road north of Rue du Bacquerot. XLII and VI Brigade howitzer batteries were located hereabouts and, as a main access route, the road was constantly repaired.

and 4 Companies of 2/2 Gurkhas emerged from their parapets to form up. From a range of less than 150 yards inescapable concentrated fire opened up from the German parapet – rifle and heavy machine gun - to cut the leading ranks to pieces before they even crossed the few yards to the ditch ahead. To their left the Seaforths, standing to advance, fell under a sudden similar hail of bullets, fire from the opposing breastworks being augmented by a continuous stream of machine gun fire from a strong point at the corner of the Bois du Biez.

As the tattered remnants of the lead companies struggled amongst their disabled and dead, only the remainder of No 4 Company 2/2Gurkhas succeeded in any forward movement.

Lieutenant-Colonel TW Gilbert, 1/4 Seaforths, recognising the impossibility of the situation, ordered all to take cover and went to advise Colonel Boileau, commanding 2/2 Gurkhas, of his order and the situation. However, just after his departure, having received no counter instruction, No 3 Company emerged over the parapet to run forward in support of No 4 Company directly into the same hail of bullets, and death.

The War Diary of the 1 /4 Seaforth Highlanders (4th Ross Highland Territorial Battalion) is written on small sheets of square ruled paper and the section covering the action of 9 May is missing.

May 1 of the War Diary records 'an exciting incident – the barn occupied by G Company went on fire. Barn completely gutted out and most of outhouses – livestock etc., and farmhouse saved'. A mere shadow of the excitement that was very shortly to follow.

On 4 May all Officers, Sergeant Majors, and Quartermaster and platoon Sergeants convened to hear a paper by General Haking entitled, 'the attack in trench warfare' read by the Commanding Officer. On 5 May, No 1 Company, with two machine guns, preceded the rest of the battalion to take up forward positions to the left of 6/Jats in the orchard.

At about 11 pm on the 8th May the rest of the battalion moved up to assemble in the attack trenches, A and C Companies leading, with B and G Companies in immediate support.

Second Lieutenant AHC Hope recorded his experience of events in his private diary.

At 5.30 a.m. A and C companies were over the parapet with B and G (second line) few minutes later. Very heavy fire – advance quite out of question. Of officers wounded, Railton and MacDonald (badly), Cameron (severe shoulder wounds), Knight, Pender, and Watt – slightly. Killed or believed killed

Bastian and Charles Tennant. Railton was missed by stretcher-bearers and found two days later killed by shrapnel. Battalion relieved 4 p.m. – to St Vaast post. Arrived Riez Bailleul via Estaires 8 p.m. One third of Battalion killed or wounded.

1/Seaforth Highlanders, commanded by Lieutenant-Colonel AB Ritchie, had relieved 2/Gurkhas in the sector trenches on 5 May, 2/ Leicesters and 6/Jats of the Garhwal Brigade to their left, and 4/Seaforths to the right. On 6th May the Battalion Diary records that eight men were wounded, two of whom died of wounds, when shellfire struck billets, and four men of A Company received incapacitating wounds in the trenches – two subsequently died. On 8 May, B, C and D Companies, in battle order, left their billets to assume their allotted assault positions astride the La Bassée to Estaires road south of Port Arthur. They were lead by B Company, allotted 150 yards to the east of the road, with C Company in a reclaimed fire trench, behind them D Company in Crescent Trench, with A Company in Pioneer Trench. Under the thunder of the opening bombardment, at 5.25 am B and C Companies went over the parapet to line out and advance. The battalion diary noted, 'even during the bombardment maxims were fired and considerable rifle fire'.

The same pattern was repeated all along the 800 yards wide front, the number of dead and injured mounting by the second with forward progress negligible.

Within twenty minutes of the start of the attack on the southern front, the right side of the pincer movement, total failure of the great opening assault was obvious. The 2 and 3 Brigades had lost 83 officers and 2135 men killed, wounded, and missing, and the Dehra Dun Brigade 37 officers and 856 other ranks killed and wounded. No objectives had been reached, the front line was not advanced at all, and very little damage had been inflicted on the enemy. Lieutenant-General Anderson advised his Corps Commander of the total failure of the two assaults by the Indian Corps and after a brief discussion a further attack was planned.

At about 7 a.m. Brigadier General Jacob, commanding the Dehra Dun Brigade, ordered his lead battalions to attack again to coincide with another attempt by the 1st Division.

After a further bombardment starting at 7.45 am and lasting for an hour, 2/2 Gurkhas and the Seaforths would attack with two companies of the 1/9 Gurkhas supporting 1/4 Seaforths, and their other two companies the severely depleted 1/Seaforths.

The result of the bombardment was that an intense answering

artillery barrage fell on the forward and reserve positions, causing extensive casualties and interrupting forward movement by the supporting 1/9 Gurkhas.

The two lead platoons of D and A Companies 1/Seaforths crossed the parapet to be again cut down within a few yards, the same fate befalling the final platoons pushed into the unremitting maelstrom of fire.

Alongside the Seaforths, the leading company of 2/2 Gurkhas rose to advance at the double. Major Rooke, urging his troops forward, was shot almost immediately, but his men, joined by others who had been pinned down in No Man's Land by the unabating fire, rushed on towards the German line. Cut down and dwindling rapidly in number as they ran, the company perished in the unsupported attack. The last remaining few, divested of all other equipment, stormed the enemy trenches and attacked the enemy with kukris. Hopelessly outnumbered, all were killed in close range combat and, with due tribute to their bravery, were communally buried behind the lines that evening by the German defenders. Wounded comrades lay out where they fell to wait amongst the dead, trapped and easy targets for German grenades.

On being advised by 1st Division Headquarters that 2 and 3 Brigades had also failed in their attacks and that any further action would only be possible after some hours of reorganisation, General Anderson cancelled the 8.45 am attack, but not until 9 am was the order to retire passed forward. Few were able to return – many lay out until the afternoon attack by the Bareilly Brigade afforded opportunity, others returned after dark. German artillery maintained a sustained barrage of HE and shrapnel fire on the front and support trenches throughout the day.

At about 2 pm 41st Dogras arrived to relieve 1/Seaforths. Those able withdrew to breastworks near Croix Barbee and, about 8 pm, retired to billets at Riez Bailleul.

Roll call revealed that twenty one officers and 488 other ranks were lost. The dead are named as: Captain DH Davidson; Captain AB Baillie Hamilton; Lieutenant JAG Inglis (4/ HLI); and Second Lieutenants J Hemingway, AEJ Shackleford, DAH McDougall, D Marion, and D Marvin. The wounded are listed as Captain R Horn (Adjutant); Lieutenants RH Allanby and A Irvine; Lieutenant GE Wakefield (3/Scots Fus); and Second Lieutenants D Lindsay, JA St L Tredennick, PH Gummings, IM Matheson, FH Maitland, and IG Barclay(shock).

6/Jats, holding the front line between the 1st Division and the Indian Brigade attacks, registered the loss of two officers and fifty two men.

1/9 Gurkha Rifles had been billeted at Vielle Chapelle from where working parties helped prepare forward positions from 6 May. Lieutenant Collins supervised a fatigue of 100 men laying cables as directed by the Divisional Signals Officers whilst 200 men under Lieutenant Taylor and Second Lieutenant Duncan worked as directed by 6/Jats HQ (96 Piccadilly) digging communication trenches. On 8 May at 8.30 pm, HQ and No. 4 Company moved forward, followed at ten minute intervals by No. 3 Company to reinforce the 1/Seaforths, No. 1 Company to reinforce 4/Seaforths, then No. 2 Company to act as general support. With the Seaforths attack arrested in front of the breastworks, one platoon of No. 3 Company, lead by Sub Mehar Suig Khattri, and two platoons from, No. 1 Company lead by Captain Pike, forced themselves into the melee around 7 am but were unable to make progress. Shells exploded in and around the forward trenches continually throughout the morning, causing heavy casualties. At 11.30 am the CO was advised that his battalion was to be relieved by troops of the Bareilly Brigade who would mount an afternoon attack. Having moved back with great difficulty to reserve breastworks east of Lansdowne Post, the battalion marched back to billets near Vielle Chapelle. Roll call revealed eight men had been killed and 111 wounded.

Behind the 2/2 Gurkhas, Lieutenant-Colonel Drake-Brockman's two battalion strong special force, comprised of 2/8 Gurkhas and 39th Garhwal Rifles (an amalgamation of the remainders of two battalions that had originally arrived in France), formed up ready to cover the left flank of the Indian Corps advance, to form a defensive flank along the right of the Bois du Biez, and then to capture and secure the German strongpoint known as La Russie at the north east corner of the wood.

The 2/8 Gurkhas were transferred to the Garhwal Brigade from the Bareilly Brigade on 31st January 1915 after completing a journey to the Western Front that started in Port Said on 6 October 1914. They were similarly to return en route to Mesopotamia in the autumn of 1915.

Their Battalion Diary records:
arrived Marseilles 12 Oct 1914 and entrained on the 18th

Gurkhas on the move.

*with 13 British officers, 17 Gurkha officers, 730 other ranks, 12
machine gun mules, 34 transport mules, 9 AT carts, 14 transport
carts, 24 public followers, and 18 private followers.*
They left Marseilles at 10.21 am on 19th en route to Orleans, where
they detrained at 4.30 pm on 21 Oct. Tents were pitched and a rest
camp established. On 26th the battalion again entrained, leaving
Orleans at 5 am the following morning to arrive in Thiennes at 5 pm
on 28th, where the companies formed up and marched to Robecq (nine
miles south of Hazebrouck). After one day in billets they moved on to
Gorre (2 miles south of Bethune), where a three-hour halt was called,
before the eastwards march resumed to arrive, on 29 Oct, west of
Festubert and into trenches straddling La Quinque Rue.

The diary records 'this place [Festubert] was shelled by German
artillery and the church caught fire about 11 p.m'. Between then and 8
May1915, through the cold damp winter of 1914/15, the battalion
remained on front line roster duties, registering the loss of six British
officers killed and three wounded, including the C.O., Lieutenant-
Colonel Morris. Of the Gurkha officers, two were killed and two
missing, and rank and file lost 37 killed, 61 wounded and 109 were
posted missing.

On 9 May 1915 the battalion moved from bivouacs in Loretto in file
of company, No. 1 Company leading, followed by No. 3, then 4, then
2, to form up behind the 2/2 Gurkhas in shallow trenches without
parapets or parados where, lying flat on their stomachs, the men
endured an intense shrapnel counter barrage starting from 5.30 am and
intermittent shelling and regular machine gun strafings for the next
twelve hours. The collapse of the successive assault attempts ahead
rendered their special mission superfluous. Major Cassels, Captain
Buckland DSO, Captain Skene, and Captain Chesney, Jemadar
Dhanbir Thapa, and Jemadars Kirta Singh Pan, and Parbir Thapa were
injured, and of rank and file three were killed and seventy eight
wounded including the SAS Bhat Nagar. The battalion spent 10 May
clearing dead and wounded from the front and communication
trenches, and there they remained to make good and hold the line.

39th Garhwalis had moved from trenches near Neuve Chapelle, to
arrive on 5 May at 3.30 a.m. to billet in two large farms on the Loretto
road. HRH Prince of Wales paid an informal visit on the afternoon of
6th, to the great delight of both officers and men. Battalion officers
reconnoitred the battlefront later in the day.

In the evening of 8 May, with the muffled sound of the French
bombardment at Vimy clearly booming across the land from the south,

the battalion marched in battle order to their allotted assembly point. Passing the crossroads at Port Arthur at 10 pm and turning north, they accessed a communication trench to their assembly trenches to the east of the Estaires road, arriving about 00.30 on 9 May.

Waiting behind 2/8 Gurkhas with shells exploding amongst them throughout the day, they waited in vain for the order to move forward. On the clear fine day of 10 May the battalion moved into the front line trenches, to hold the line to the left of 2/Leicesters.

Major Woods had been killed and Captain Berryman and Second Lieutenant Saunders wounded by shell fragments; Subradar Gopi Sing Rarrat, and Jemadars Pancham Sing Mahar, Teg Sing Kaphola, Jura Sing Negi and Kashi Sing Negi, were wounded, and two other ranks were killed and 94 wounded during the long day's wait.

By 8 am, from liaison officers and from Divisional Headquarters, General Haig had received reports of the poor progress, but these messages failed to convey sufficiently the extent of the enormous losses incurred without gain, and orders to reorganise in readiness for a further full scale attack at noon were issued. Only after visiting General Willcocks at the Indian Corps Headquarters at Lestrem and learning that the Dehra Dun Brigade had been so damaged that any further participation by them was out of the question and the Bareilly Brigade would have to replace them, did Haig postpone until 2.40 pm his plan to assault again with 1st Division and Indian Division troops. The order was again delayed due to difficulties in moving brigades in daylight whilst receiving the full attention of the German artillery and assembling the battalions in badly damaged and congested trenches filled with dead and wounded. Zero hour for a further assault from the Rue du Bois front was re-scheduled for 4.00 pm.

C. IV Corps. The attack towards Rouge Bancs and Fromelles (Northern front).

IV Corps, between Neuve Chapelle and Bois Grenier, faced four regiments of the 6th Bavarian Reserve Division. From south to north the regiments were: 17th Reserve, 16th Reserve, 21st Reserve, and 20th Reserve. Each German regiment had a fighting strength of 33 officers, 160 NCOs and 1970 men, and each was divided into twelve companies, six of which rotated front line duties with the other six who were billeted, in reserve, some 2500 metres behind the lines.

The plan of Lieutenant-General Rawlinson was to attack towards Rouges Bancs on a 1200 metre front across the Sailly to Fromelles road. On this frontage, six companies of the 16th, and four companies

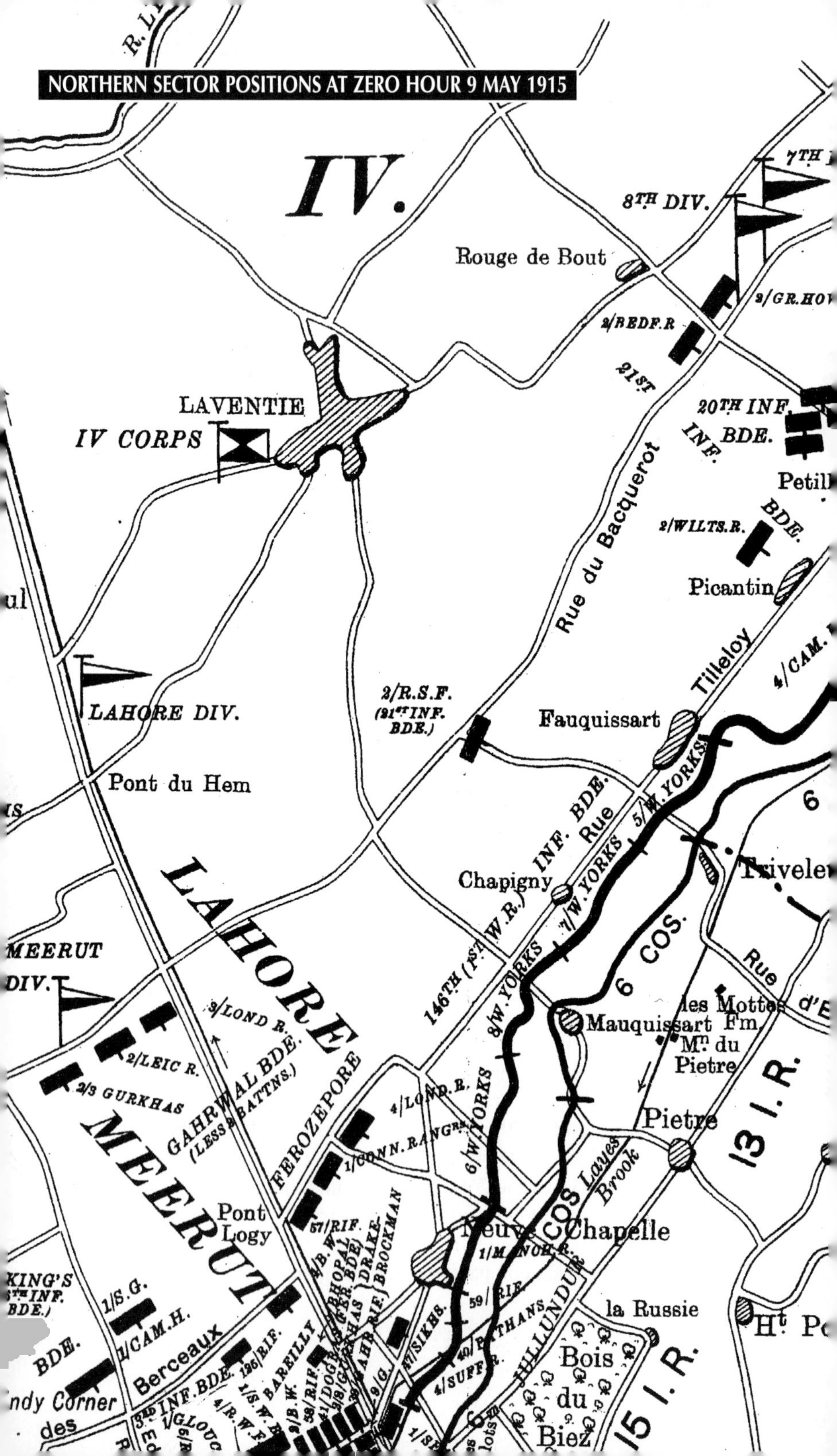

IV.

8TH DIV.

7TH

Rouge de Bout

2/REDF.R.

2/GR.HOW

21ST

20TH INF.
BDE.

Petil

LAVENTIE

IV CORPS

2/WILTS.R.

Rue du Bacquerot

BDE.

Picantin

Tilleloy

4/CAM.

LAHORE DIV.

2/R.S.F.
(21ST INF.
BDE.)

Fauquissart

Pont du Hem

5/W.YORKS

Chapigny

7/W.YORKS

Trivele

MEERUT
DIV.

146TH (3/W.R.)

INF. BDE.
Rue

6 COS.

Rue

2/LEIC R.

3/LOND R.

les Mottes
Mauquissart Fm
Mn du
Pietre

131 I.R.

2/3 Gurkhas

GAHRWAL BDE.
(LESS 2 BATTNS.)

8/W.YORKS

FEROZEPORE

4/LOND. R.

6 COS.

Pietre

KING'S
INF.
BDE.

1/CONN. RANGERS

6/W.YORKS

Layes

Brook

Pont
Logy

57/RIF.

1/MANCH R.

COS. Chapelle

la Russie

Ht Po

Berceaux

59

4/SUFF.

HILLUNDUR

Bois
du
Biez

151 I.R.

ndy Corner
des

1/S.G.

1/CAM.H.

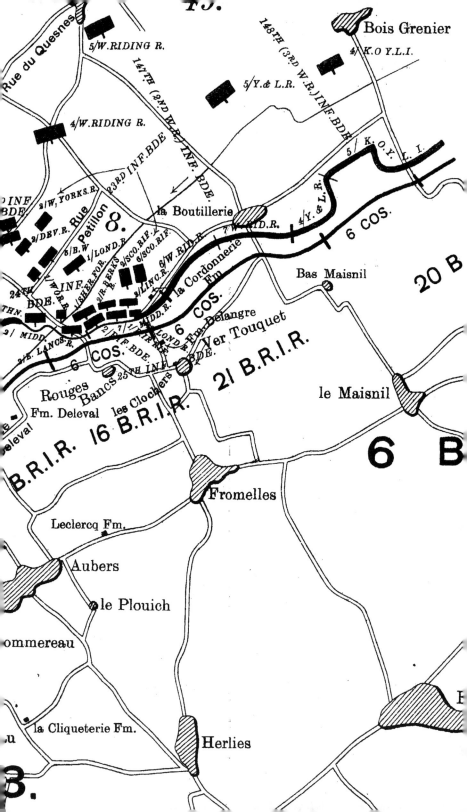

NORTHERN SECTOR ARTILLERY BOMBARDMENT 9 MAY 1915

NOTE. ARRANGEMENTS FOR THE 1ST PHASE
OF THE BOMBARDMENT (5.-5.50 A.M.)

15" HOWS. bombarding Fromelles & Aubers.

9·2" HOWS. shelling Fm. Deleval & selected points.

6" HOWS. bombarding German Front Line.

4·5" HOWS. bombarding the 3 front German trenches.

4·7" GUNS. bombarding selected points, searching specified areas, & sweeping Fromelles ridge, also shelling Fournes & chateau.

18-PDR. Q.F. Wire-cutting (5.-5.15); bombarding German front trench, & sweeping back.

13-PDR. Q.F. shelling selected points, searching communication trenches.

15-PDR. B.L.C. shelling selected area.

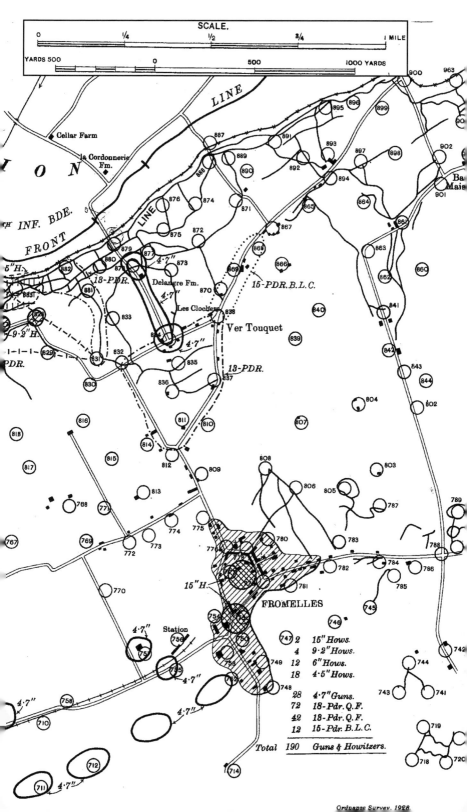

SCALE.

0   1/4   1/2   3/4   1 MILE

YARDS 500   0   500   1000 YARDS

Cellar Farm

la Cordonnerie Fm.

LINE

FRONT LINE

INF. BDE.

5" H.

13-PDR.

4·7"

Delangre Fm.

4·7"

Les Clochers

Ver Touquet

4·7"

13-PDR.

15-PDR.B.L.C.

9·2" H.

PDR.

15" H.

FROMELLES

Station

4·7"

4·7"

4·7"

4·7"

Ba Maie

2	15" Hows.	
4	9·2" Hows.	
12	6" Hows.	
18	4·5" Hows.	
28	4·7" Guns.	
72	18-Pdr. Q.F.	
42	18-Pdr. Q.F.	
12	15-Pdr. B.L.C.	

Total   190   *Guns & Howitzers.*

Ordnance Survey. 1928.

The British armoured train – May 1915.

of the 21st Regiment, totalling about 1600 defenders, faced the attack of 24 and 25 Brigades - some 7000 men.

The 8th Division, commanded by Major-General FJ Davies, was to advance eastwards to Fromelles, and the 7th Division, under the command of Major-General H de la P Gough, would follow through, to attack south eastwards with Aubers and Leclercq Farm as objectives. The intention was that the 7th Division would continue towards La Plouich and La Cliqueterie Farm on Aubers Ridge (where they would link with the Indian Corps to seal the front and enclose the enemy). The 8th Division would defend the flank thus formed from Fromelles to La Cordonnerie Farm (half a mile north of Rouge Bancs).

The bombardment preceding the attack on the northern front was undertaken by No. 2 Group H.A.R. under the command of Brigadier-General HCC Uniacke and the 7th and 8th Division artilleries plus VII Siege Brigade, all under the command of Brigadier-General AEA Holland – a total of 190 field guns and howitzers.

Heavy howitzer fire was to be directed against the fortified farms of Deleval and Delangre, and the German batteries along the crest of Aubers Ridge and around the villages of Aubers and Fromelles. The 49th (West Riding) Division artillery shelled the German trenches on the immediate right of the attack to deter lateral action against advancing troops.

No. 2 Group H.A.R. was to destroy specific strong points beyond the range of the divisional artillery and to eliminate four Bavarian

The northern attack front – viewed from the German front trench line.

24 BRIGADE

1/WORCS
2/NORTHANTS
2/EAST LANCS

1/5 SHERWOOD FORESTERS

8TH DIVISION FRONT

2/RIFLE BRIGADE

Heavy batteries around Herlies and Fournes and twelve field batteries of the 6th Bavarian Reserve Division near Aubers, Fromelles, and Le Maisnil. No. 2 Group consisted of: two 15 inch howitzers of R.M.A.; two 9.2 inch howitzers of 12th Siege Battery; two 9.2 inch howitzers of 13th Siege Battery; ten 4.7 inch guns of III Heavy Brigade; ten 4.7 inch guns of VIII Heavy Brigade; four 4.7 inch guns of 1st West Riding Heavy Battery; four 4.7 inch guns of 1st Highland Heavy Battery; and the armoured trains, 'Churchill' manned by naval gunners and 'Deguise' manned by Belgian artillerymen, with two 6 inch guns, two 4.7 inch guns, and a 4 inch gun.

German breastworks and forward positions were to be pounded by twelve 6 inch howitzers of VII Siege Brigade and eighteen 4.5 inch divisional howitzers, whilst 72 18-pdr guns cut wire. Seven R.H.A 13-pdr batteries were to sweep communication trenches and block into isolation the forward German trenches.

On 24 Brigade front, two guns of the 104th Battery, XXII Brigade, R.F.A., fitted with rubber rimmed wheels, were stealthily brought forward during the night into specially prepared front line emplacements under orders to breach the barbed wire defences fronting the salient which was to be attacked by the 2/Northants on the right and 2/East Lancs on the left. One gun tore several gaps through the barbed wire – the other was rendered completely ineffective as weak flooring shattered and collapsed.

During the night of 8/9 May, Major-General FJ Davies moved 24 and 25 Brigades into the 1200 yards wide attack front, the line held by 2/Middx and 1/7Middx of 23 Brigade. The remaining four battalions of 23 Brigade were held in divisional reserve, ready to push through the assaulting battalions as soon as their first objectives were achieved, and 20 and 22 Brigades of the 7th Division were assembled a mile to the rear of the 8th Division. 21 Brigade (less two battalions with the 49th Division) was held in Corps reserve behind them.

Men from 2/East Lancs of 24 Brigade, under Major H Maclean, led on the right flank with, on their left, 25 Brigade, 2/Rifle Brigade under Lieutenant-Colonel RB Stephens, and 1/Royal Irish Rifles commanded

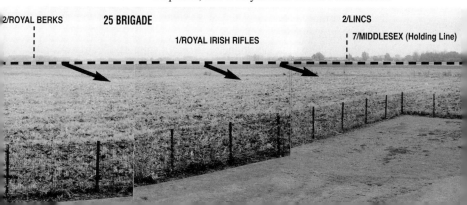

2/ROYAL BERKS   **25 BRIGADE**   2/LINCS

1/ROYAL IRISH RIFLES   7/MIDDLESEX (Holding Line)

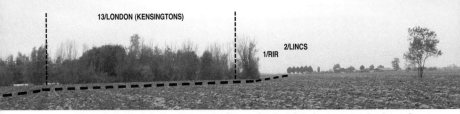

Viewed from La Cordonnerie farm the British front stretched to about where now stands VC Cemetery, visible at the line of trees on the horizon. 13/London Regt (The Kensingtons) were some 400 yards away from the left flank of the attacking 1/Royal Irish Rifles, 2/Lincolns holding reserve trenches between the two battalions.

by Lieutenant-Colonel OC Baker (who died in action). These three assault battalions attacked across a 700 yards wide front over the Rue Delvas towards Rouges Bancs.

Substantial subsidiary attacks pressed forward on either side of this main force. On the right flank, 2/Northants mounted an assault to the south west against the exposed German salient and, 400 yards to the left of the main front, 1/13 London Regiment (The Kensingtons), commanded by Lieutenant-Colonel FG Lewis, attacked following the detonation of two large mines under the German front trenches opposite.

The width of No Man's Land in front of 2/Rifle Brigade and 1/RIR was about 120 yards, even less in front of 1/13 London Regiment on the left flank, but, on the right, up to 300 yards faced 2/East Lancs who were to secure the flank alongside which the subsidiary attack of 2/Northants would have to cross more than 300 yards of open ground to secure their objective.

At 3 am on the morning of the battle, whilst the British assault battalions were assembling in their forward positions, on the German side the reserve 3rd Battalion of the Bavarian Reserve Infantry Regiment, under the command of Major von Luneschloss, was replacing the 1st Battalion, which had held the line since 1st May. Their battalion diary records the transfer was undetected by the enemy and without incident. The opening onslaught would start a mere two hours later!

The British plan was that, after breakthrough, the ridge between Aubers and Fromelles was to be occupied. 24 Brigade was to secure Deleval Farm and the Rue Deleval on the right flank of the advance, and 25 Brigade to capture Fromelles and secure the left flank running from that village to la Cordonnerie Farm. In support, 23 Brigade, plus a brigade of the 7th Division under the command of Brigadier-General RJ Pinney, would advance through the gap opened by the assault attack and move south eastwards towards Aubers village and Leclercq Farm. The 7th Division brigade was then to press the advance to La Plouich

Farm, beyond Aubers and La Cliqueterie Farm, to join there the left flank of the Meerut Division, trapping the German positions thus encircled.

Troops of 23 Brigade held this section of the British front line on 9 May. On 8 May 2/Middlesex moved up to a position one mile west of the Sailly to Fromelles road on the Rue de Quesnes, to relieve and exchange billets with 2/Devons. Under the British bombardments at 5.40 am and the second short barrage at 9 am they held the trenches outside 24 and 25 Brigade attack sectors throughout the day and night of 9 May, blasted by continual and often heavy counter barrages from the German field batteries. Fourteen other ranks were killed, sixty five wounded, and two missing, and Second Lieutenant AL Bishop suffered incapacitating wounds. The battalion continued duty in the front line until 8.30 am on 13 May when 2/Devons returned to relieve the battalion and again assumed defence of the front line.

Billeted one and a half miles north west of Sailly since 4 May, 2/East Lancs received an order to move at 10 pm on 7 May to assembly trenches on the Fromelles to Sailly road opposite Rouge Bancs. A message received at 5 pm on the 7th ordered the battalion to stand fast for twenty-four hours and the battalion started their delayed move forward at 10 pm on 8 May, to assemble in attack order, in the forward trenches behind the breastworks.

C and B Companies would lead the assault with D Company in immediate support and A Company held back in reserve.

2/East Lancs plan of attack, on the right flank of the main 24 Brigade front, was shattered almost before it began. Attacking into conditions repeatedly reported along the whole front, the lead platoons emerging over the parapet came 'immediately under very heavy machine gun crossfire losing heavily even before crossing the Fromelles Road' (the Rue Delvas).

Regrouping, the leading companies, with D Company now following directly behind, doubled forward when the bombardment lifted at 5.40 am but were, 'again mown down before they had gone twenty five yards, the survivors creeping back as best they could to the trench and sap on Fromelles Road'.

Progress being impossible, a further artillery bombardment was requested and those remaining of the battalion regrouped in forward trenches behind the scant shelter of the breastworks in preparation for another attempt to reach the German defences scheduled for 7.30 am.

Brigadier-General Oxley, on learning of the debacle, immediately ordered forward two companies of the supporting 1/Sherwood

Viewed from behind Le Trou Cemetery – reserve troop positions a.m. 9 May 1915.

Foresters. In spite of the carnage and confusion in the forward area, they managed to follow up the attack at 6.10 am.

The War Diary of 2/East Lancs reads –

Bombardment but shells falling short into the Fromelles trench, in the parapet, in rear, and in the assembly trenches behind the parapet. As the Regiment was being rapidly annihilated by our own artillery it was withdrawn behind the parapet to the West side of Fromelles Road (1P & 1Q).

The attempt to overcome concentrated machine gun and rifle cross fire by massed attackers had been proven a total waste, as had been feared and voiced by some field commanders.

The failure of their assault was officially explained in their War Diary as:

(a) Distance of 300 yards to cross.

(b) Assembly trench at right angles to objective thus involving a left wheel.

(c) Total failure by artillery to shake the German parapet as the enemy maintained heavy rifle and machine gun fire during both bombardments.

The stated failure had resulted in ten officers killed and nine wounded, and 63 other ranks killed, 42 missing and 325 wounded.

The dead officers were: Major L Russell, Captain WF Richardson, Lieutenant JH Daw, Second Lieutenants E Bligh, GML Goodall, HE Howell, AG Norton, PHC Allen, AE Dothie, and AP Marshall. The wounded were: Captain KHL Arnott (Adjutant), Lieutenant RS Boothby, and Second Lieutenants RK Cannan, L Andersson, HL Owen, EJ Henderson, WO Heape, HT Gorst and ELA Cope.

At 1 am on 10 May the remnants of 2/East Lancs were withdrawn to bivouac and reorganise at Rue de Bout. 1/Nottinghamshire and Derbyshire Regiment (The Sherwood Foresters) had been holding the front line until relieved by 2/Scottish Rifles (The Cameronians) on 5 May, when they withdrew to billets a half a mile north of Sailly.

Starting at 10.25 pm on 8 May the battalion moved forward, without incurring casualties, to trenches 500 yards south of the Rue Petillon,

ready to support the frontal attack spearheaded by 2/East Lancs. 1/Sherwood Foresters, with B Company on the left and D Company on the right, were to follow the East Lancs as they vacated the front trenches. A and C Companies formed behind ready to press through the attack.

The lead platoons were unable to start moving until 6.10 am, delayed as troops of 2/East Lancs crumbled under the concentrated fire from eight enemy machine guns trained on their restricted exits, some from fixed positions others firing without tripods from the top of the breastworks. With the rear platoons of 2/East Lancs pinned down only twenty yards out from the forward trench, B and D Companies of the Sherwood Foresters were ordered to advance half right into fierce fire.

Although suffering extreme casualties in crossing No Man's Land the lead platoons struggled on, only to be halted by unbroken wire and were isolated some forty yards in front of the German breastworks. Only one gap of about four yards wide in the enemy wire was evident as, stranded and without shelter, those remaining of B Company were wiped out from close range. Noting that the East Lancs and some supporting Royal Berks to their left were moving back towards shelter trenches in front of the breastworks, the CO, Major Morley, also ordered the remnants of his B and D Companies to withdraw.

Corporal J Upton, 1/Sherwood Foresters, disregarding his own safety whilst under exposure to very heavy rifle and artillery fire, repeatedly crossed and re-crossed No Man's Land to rescue wounded, carried them back from within close proximity of the enemy parapet, and then treated and dressed their wounds in front of his own parapet. For displaying great courage throughout the day Corporal Upton was awarded the Victoria Cross. His medal is displayed at the Sherwood Foresters' Museum in Nottingham Castle.

At about 9.35 am, after a short local bombardment had been directed at the opposing trenchworks, A and C Companies followed by the reorganised remainder of B and D Companies, supported the regrouped 2/East Lancs in another attempt to make headway against the continuing onslaught of defensive fire. The attack again ground to a halt some fifty yards into No Man's Land. With units disorganised and broken, those who were able once again scrambled back to the shelter of the breastworks, leaving many more stranded to seek whatever cover they could find.

The Sherwood Foresters War Diary records '11.00 am – Captain Young B Company and 5 others wounded by shell. Half of A company still lying in the open'.

At 5.45 am, before 1/Sherwood Foresters were ordered forward, and unaware that the covering advance of the 2/East Lancs, 500 yards to their left, had been brought to an abrupt halt by the withering fire, 2/Northants, in accordance with their orders, rose to attack the fortified salient guarded by 8 Company, 16 Bavarian (Reserve) Regiment.

From 4 to 8 May 2/Northants had been billeted a mile west of Sailly preparing and training for the offensive and, after the last minute 24 hour delay, followed 1/5 Black Watch in column of route, to arrive in their assembly trenches at thirty minutes past midnight on 9 May.

D Company, commanded by Lieutenant OK Parker, had preceded the battalion move forward and, during the night, had prepared the way for the lead assault platoons by clearing access paths through the British wire and digging shallow shelter trenches beyond, then withdrawing to the Orchard to join up with A Company, commanded by Captain Ward-Hunt. B Company was assembled in trenches behind the Orchard with C Company to their right. From the jumping off trenches, the battalion had in excess of 300 yards of open ground to cross to reach the trenches opposite.

104 Battery, XXII Brigade, RFA, using two of their field guns from positions in the breastworks during the opening bombardment, were reported to have blown a number of gaps through the wire guarding the front of the German salient.

The bombardment on the salient, point 372, continued for ten minutes longer than the main artillery barrage and, at 5.50 am, as the guns lifted, A Company on the left, and D Company on the right, started their horrific struggle to advance across the waste of No Man's Land. Continuous machine gun fire tearing at their left flank, A Company fought through to the enemy barbed wire but, unable to find a way through, were there trapped and all the men remaining were wiped out by short range machine gun and rifle fire. About thirty men of D Company, lead by Lieutenant Parker, found a way through the enemy wire and scrambling over the breastworks captured a stretch of trench only to be immediately pinned down by showers of grenades. At 6 am, B Company, lead by Lieutenant Middleton, tried to progress in support of A Company but was quickly brought to a standstill.

The 2/Northants crossed over 300 yards of No Man's Land towards Aubers' church spire to attack the German Salient.

Following at 6.25 am, C Company, lead by Captain Jackson, under cover of fire from two machine guns directed by Lieutenant Lawrence, attempted to fight through to reinforce the small bridgehead established by Lieutenant Parker and his men. This stretch of No Man's Land had by this time become an impenetrable curtain of machine gun, rifle and artillery fire. No more troops were able to reach the enemy lines. Tangled remains of trees and bushes restricted the view across the torn ground and visual communication with Lieutenant Parker's isolated party became impossible.

Private Lapham, 2/Northants, answered the call for a volunteer to attempt a lone crossing of No Man's Land to determine the situation and position of the men trapped with Lieutenant Parker. Snaking and crawling from hole to hole through mud and amidst explosions, and under very heavy rifle fire, he miraculously returned to report that about thirty men were alive and holding out. As the day progressed the squad was forced back over the German parapet but reformed in a line of shell holes fronting the breastworks from where they returned fire although being constantly bombed.

All British forward positions continued to be heavily shelled throughout the day and well into the following night.

At 8 pm, under the cover of darkness, Lieutenant Parker and four men stumbled back into the British lines, followed 'a little later' by Sergeant Brightman leading nine men and ten walking wounded. Stretcher-bearers worked all night to recover 'large numbers of wounded' from No Man's Land.

At about 9.15 pm the remainder of 2/Northants were ordered back to the divisional reserve trenches south of the Rue de Bout and left the support trenches as soon as relieved by a company of 1/Worcesters at around 2.45 am on 10 May. Casualties had reduced the battalion strength from 887men to 441.

Of A Company Captain G Ward-Hunt and Second Lieutenant B Eden were dead, Lieutenant CD Beresford wounded and Second

Lieutenant GF Blacker missing; of B Company only Second Lieutenant GR Friendship was unhurt, Lieutenant AD Middleton and Second Lieutenants AM Eldridge and JT Peake were wounded, and of C Company, Second Lieutenant E Mason was dead, Captain HW Jackson wounded, and only Second Lieutenants JA Ellerman and HW Carritt remained unscathed. In D Company Lieutenant OK Parker was unhurt in spite of his fifteen hours of exposure in the midst of the frantic action, but Second Lieutenant RW Randall was missing and Second Lieutenant DW Ryan dead. Second Lieutenant CH Viney, the bomb party officer, was reported missing and his body was never recovered. Lieutenant CC Court, the RAMC medical officer, and Lieutenant FH Lawrence, the machine gun officer, were uninjured. Lieutenant Parker, for his exceptional gallantry, was awarded the Military Cross.

Casualties amongst other ranks totalled 63 dead, 197 missing and unaccounted for and 154 wounded. At 2.25 am on 11 May 2/Northants left the divisional reserve trenches and withdrew to billets in Laventie.

1/5 Black Watch (Royal Highlanders), a territorial battalion, as reserve battalion ordered to follow up the initial attacks, moved into rear assembly trenches ahead of 1/Worcesters. After a full fighting order inspection by their CO, the battalion had followed 2/East Lancs to arrive at assembly trenches opposite Brigade HQ in the Rue Petillon just after midnight.

When the bombardment concluded, the reserve battalions started forward to assume their follow up attack positions in the fire trenches but, due to confusion and overcrowding, 1/5 Black Watch were instead forced to occupy forward assembly and communication trenches close to where Riviere des Laies crossed the trench line. The War diary states

From Rue Petillon forward the battalion suffered badly from machine gun and artillery fire, and that the move forward was checked by Sherwood Foresters being unable to vacate fire trenches.

The battalion waited in the assembly trenches during the morning 'suffering casualties from heavy enemy shellfire', and at 1 pm, as the British bombardment started, so did the consternation in the ranks as 'short falling shells caused many more casualties'.

The battalion, having been under continual bombardment throughout the day, was ordered back to divisional reserve at 10 pm. Assembling by company at the crossroads on the Rue du Quesnes, the battalion then marched to bivouac in le Rouge de Bout just north of the crossroads, arriving at about 1.30 am on 10 May 1915. Eight

Men of the Black Watch in a machine gun emplacement. The 'dangerous' sign a stark reminder of the risk from sniper fire.

officers had been wounded, and 22 other ranks killed, six were missing, and 108 wounded.

The wounded officers were Captain T Aubertin, Lieutenants RFD Bruce, AD Dickie, AW Duke, and HR McCabe, and Second Lieutenants HS Quekett, RM Richie and (registered as accidental!) the Hon. T Bowes-Lyon, brother of the future Queen.

On 2 May 1915 Major Arden DSO had taken over as Second in Command of the 1 /Worcestershire Regt, and at 10.50 pm 8 May, led the march from billets in Sailly to arrive, as the second reserve battalion to support the initial attack, in the assembly trenches on Rue de Petillon, at 1.30 am on 9 May.

Subjected to continual shellfire during the move forward, D and B Companies with two machine guns were, by 6.15 am, positioned immediately to the rear of 2/East Lancs and 1/Sherwood Foresters, ready to press forward in support of those assaulting battalions. Following some 400 yards behind, A and C Companies with another two machine guns entrenched behind the Rue Petillon. A Company had veered off course during the forward move and, having arrived to the right of 2/East Lancs, had to realign their position.

The repulse of the first assaults prevented early participation as planned and the battalion waited for fresh orders. Between 9 and 9.15 am a short barrage was concentrated on the German lines and having moved forward at 9.20 am, A Company on the right, and C Company to the left, attempted to move into the breastworks. They were barely able to pass through the mess and confusion of corpses and wounded in the wrecked forward trenches, and the front trench was unreachable through the congestion. The War diary states,

By 9.30 am second attempt had come to a standstill. Wounded blocking communication trenches in rear.

The morning assault of 2/East Lancs and 1/Sherwood Foresters in front of 1/Worcesters had ground to a halt, and 24 Brigade attack was thereby terminated.

Sustained rifle and machine gun fire with artillery bombardments from both sides persisted throughout the morning, with steadily increasing numbers of casualties.

At 12.50 an order was received by 1/Worcesters HQ that, with the regrouped 1/Sherwood Foresters in support, the battalion was to attack at 1.30 pm.

The Commanding Officer, whilst preparing to attack, referred back to 24 Brigade Headquarters stating that in his opinion an attack could not succeed and that he would await formal confirmation of the order before proceeding. His stated reasons were:

1. Great crowding and confusion in breastworks – proper deployment not possible.

2. Only small parties could emerge at any one time – concerted attack not possible.

3. Same circumstances would apply to the supporting troops.

4. Due to above rapid attack rendered impossible.

and last, but by no means least,

5. In spite of our bombardment, [enemy] *fire of the most intense imaginable is being sustained.*

At 12.55 the War Diary notes an *'Increased intensity of enfilade fire into the left of battalion'.*

The planned 1.30 pm attack did not take place and, as other troops were withdrawn, the battalion was deployed in order of company A, D, C and B, along the 600 yard stretch of the British front line from Sailly - Fromelles road (Riviere des Laies). They remained holding the line until relieved by 2/Middlesex and 2/Scottish Rifles at 10.30 pm on 11

May, when they returned to billets in Laventie. During the three days on station the battalion lost one officer killed, three wounded and one incapacitated due to shellshock; and of the NCOs and men, 31 were killed, eight posted as missing believed dead, and 185 wounded.

To the left of the 24 Brigade, 25 Brigade commanded by Brigadier-General Lowry Cole simultaneously attacked the front to the east of the Sailly – Fromelles road.

2/Rifle Brigade and 1/Royal Irish Rifles lead the brigade assault against 9 Company, 16th Bavarian (Reserve) Infantry Regiment holding the trench lines opposite.

Although the German breastworks a hundred yards ahead seemed much damaged, fire from the German trenches here was still of shocking intensity, cutting into the lead companies as they clambered over the parapets to attack. Hurrying determinedly forward in lines of platoon thirty paces apart, the surviving troops found the wire successfully severed and a wide breach in the breastworks allowed them to storm into the opposing trenches. Casualties amongst the defenders as a result of the bombardment had in fact been extreme and the rapid advance secured eighty yards of German front trench. Regrouping, the attackers pressed on to secure their second objective – the road from Rouges Bancs to Fromelles some 200 yards ahead. The strong point at Rouge Bancs, from which at least two machine guns and considerable rifle fire was sustained, was attacked, and a defensive line formed to await the arrival of reinforcements.

In spite of very heavy losses, the supporting two companies of 2/Rifle Brigade struggled across through a hail of bullets and fought and bombed along the flanking trenches to widen the breach to 250 yards. However, following up behind, two companies of 2/Lincolnshires were pinned down in front of their own parapet by the desperately intense machine gun and rifle fire from the reorganised companies of 16th Bavarians in their front line trench between 1/RIR and, some 300 yards away to their left, 1/13 London Regiment.

From 5 to 8 May 1/Royal Irish Rifles had been billetted at Bac St Maur after a spell alternating front line trench duty with 2/Lincolnshires. During the march back on 5 May the noise of the cannonade resounding around Ypres was so loud as to warrant comment in their War Diary. The battalion arrived in assembly trenches at La Cordonnerie Farm at about 2 am on 9 May, then moved forward to assume attack positions.

With 2/Rifle Brigade immediately to their right and the Kensingtons away to their left, C and D Companies in lines of platoon at 30 paces, with A and B Companies following immediately behind, led the charge against heavy flanking machine gun and rifle fire. Two platoons of D Company, directed by the RSM, advanced obliquely to the left in an attempt to silence the machine guns firing into the flanks but became pinned down and, unable to progress, many were killed and wounded, and the few remaining uninjured were forced back. Storming the German lines directly ahead the forward assault platoons advanced across the German front trench and, at the track beyond, paused to await the arrival of the supporting platoons. Immediately pressured by a counter attack, and incurring losses under an onslaught of mortar and grenades, the forward troops, waiting in vain for support, were forced to withdraw back to the captured front line German trenches at about 7 am, having held their position for some thirty minutes. With all the attack officers killed, missing or wounded, the 1/Royal Irish Rifles, commanded by their RSM, with the 2/Rifle Brigade adjacent, held their section of captured trench throughout the day and into the following night until ordered to withdraw very early on 10 May. The few able bodied marched back to billets at Bac St Maur.

The sixteen officers whose deaths are recorded were: Lieutenant-Colonel OC Baker; Major AH Festing CMG DSO; Captain AM O'Sullivan B Coy; Lieutenants JS Martin, RL Neill (5/RIR), A McLoughlin (3/RIR), GM Nauze, RA Finley (5/Royal Dublin Fusiliers); and Second Lieutenants CG Dixon, AW Bourke, B McCausland, CA Windus, and D Hamilton. Lieutenant JEB Miller (5/RIR), Lieutenant LAFW Dickenson (4/Bedfordshire Regt) and Second Lieutenant A Hellmers all died from wounds. The officers wounded were: Captain CC Tae and Lieutenant RG Soulby A Coy; Lieutenants CJ Newport, SA Gray, and HP Parkes C Coy; Lieutenant GT Gartlan, Asst Adjutant and Lieutenant GM New.

Lieutenant CS Martin (5/RIR) was posted as missing. Of the rank and file, 51 had been killed, 207 wounded and 203 were missing.

2/Rifle Brigade had been billeted on Rue Bataille during the first week of May. Working parties were employed on repairing barbed wire defences by night and laying cable, under the direction of the brigade signals officer, by day. Training for the imminent battle filled all available hours. Starting their move to the allotted assembly trenches at 11 pm on 8 May the battalion formed up, with B and D Companies to lead the attack, with A and C Companies supporting. A cascade of short falling shells exploding amongst the troops in the front trench during the last ten minutes before zero hour caused severe casualties to those poised awaiting the signal to attack across No Man's Land.

German infantry counter-attack over barbed wire.

Advancing in line with the 1/RIR on their left, the waves of B and D Companies fought across against the intense fire to reach and storm over the wrecked German front trench opposite. A and C Companies and HQ with the machine guns followed as opposing fire increased to inflict very severe casualties. The machine guns failed to get across and a much dispersed HQ Company reassembled only in part. The carefully organised and practiced bombing parties were broken up during the mayhem of the crossing and their thorough training in extending the front laterally needed to be quickly revised as bombs and bombers proved difficult to locate. Scratch bombing squads secured another 50 yards to the west of the Sailly – Fromelles road and 'a bit to the east' was captured, extending the width of the breakthrough by the brigade to about 250 yards in all. Meanwhile the leading platoons of A and D Companies had pushed on until very concentrated machine gun fire from the flanks halted progress and they dug in to await reinforcements.

Lieutenant-Colonel Stevens was, at about this time, ordered back to assume brigade command after Brigadier-General Lowry-Cole had been killed in action. Nearly all the assault officers had been killed or wounded and, against increasing counter attacks and bombing from the flanks, starting at about 8 am small groups from the most forward positions began to fall back.

Lieutenant-Colonel Stephens had assigned command in the trench to Lieutenant Newport 1/RIR and crawled back to the British lines to relieve Brigadier-General Pinney and assume command of 25 Brigade. He ordered a rapid mobilisation of two bombing parties from 2/Berkshires, together with seventy 2/Rifle Brigade men with two machine guns, to cross to bolster Lieutenant Newport's party and instigated other initiatives to enable the small success to be expanded. 15 Field Company RE, commanded by Major PK Batty, was charged with the immediate task of digging a communication trench across No Man's Land to enable D Company 2/Queen's to access the ground held by Lieutenant Newport as soon as possible. In fact the unabated chaos in the wrecked front trenches prevented 2/Queen's from even reaching the access trench.

Only one of the attempts to reinforce the stranded fighters met with any success. During the morning Second Lieutenant Gray collected together about fifty riflemen from 2/Rifle Brigade and, with his party, crawled forward into an abandoned and derelict trench where they formed up ready to advance at the double. On signal they ran ahead through a hail of bullets across No Man's Land and, Lieutenant Gray with just twenty men remaining, leapt into the captured trench to join Colonel Stephens's men.

At 1.30 pm, as they waited desperately for support to enable them to advance from their trench towards their next objective, they viewed with gnawing dismay, across the Rue Delvas, the collapse of a renewed 24 Brigade attack.

German bombers persisted with their assaults against the flanks, pushing the trench blocks ever inwards. Fighting to repel successive counter attacks by the reorganised 16th Bavarians during the afternoon reduced the available bombs, ammunition and weapons, to critically low levels. Just before dusk another more concerted counter assault started. 1st Battalion 16 Bavarian (Reserve) Infantry Regiment, under the command of Major Arnold, attacked determinedly. The opening attack was broken up and repulsed with the help of rapid fire from a captured Maxim machine gun hurriedly repaired and manned by Lieutenant Gray but, as night fell, a spell of dramatic close fought action began.

From their reserve trenches between Rouges Bancs and 'the House with the White Fence' (Near point 769), Nos. 1, 3, and 4 Companies of 16th Bavarians moved off at 9.15 pm, in the dark of night, to attack and recapture the trench which had been lost that morning. Arriving, after some navigational difficulties, at the forward forming up area at about 10.15 pm, having suffered artillery casualties en route, scouts were sent out to determine the British positions. Forward patrols were posted to guide the main attack, scheduled for 1.30 am but which was re-timed for 2.45 am, following reorganisation after British artillery fire again struck the assembled attack force.

The advance in frontal attack of Nos. 1 and 3 Companies was slowed in the darkness by strafing fire from the two British machine guns. Soldiers of No 4 Company, lead by Lieutenant Gebhardt, forced entry into the right end of the British held trench and ferociously fought along the trench using hand grenades whilst the rest of the company covered the move at a tangent. Lieutenant Hock, leading a small troop of men, leapt into the trench some distance from the right extremity and pushed further along, bombing with grenades. Riflemen covering the trench clearance picked off the British infantrymen as their dark silhouettes appeared. Groups of 2/Rifle Brigade, manning blocks set up along the trench system, were bombed and, as ammunition became exhausted, the frontal assault companies overran the British positions.

At about 2.30 am on 10 May, having been fighting to hold their position since the previous dawn, with no bombs and little ammunition remaining, the remnants of the battalions were

The grave in Le Trou First Aid Post cemetery of Brigadier-General A W G, Lowry Cole CB DSO, mortally wounded whilst at the front line 9 May 1915.

finally driven out of the trench to scramble back to the British front line.

1/Royal Irish Rifles had suffered casualties totalling 477 officers and men. 2/Rifle Brigade registered nine officers killed, eight wounded and four posted missing and of the men 77 were dead, 340 wounded and 212 were missing. On arrival in Sailly at 5 am the next morning, only three officers and 195 men remained to answer the roll call.

From billets in Laventie 2/Lincolnshire Regiment had moved on 5 May to billets south east of Sailly, where they practised for the forthcoming action in support of the leading 1/Royal Irish Rifles. On 8 May the battalion marched forward to assembly trenches near the Rue Petillon, with W and X companies leading and Y and Z companies following up.

As the last of 1/RIR cleared the parapets at 5.40 am, the leading platoons of W and X companies occupied the assault trenches and then scrambled over to follow closely behind them into the tangled mess of mud and craters and the smashed detritus of battle. Dead, dying, and wounded were scattered amongst the hundreds halted by heavy artillery and intense rifle fire beyond the shallow fire trenches fronting the parapets.

Strafed by a devastating stream of machine gun bullets from the flanks, W and X companies were pinned down and stranded. Second Lieutenant Nisbet and Second Lieutenant Ayres (attached from 3/Dorsets) were killed and Lieutenant Clifford and Lieutenant Nind (3/Dorsets) severely wounded. Forward movement being impossible, Y and Z Companies were ordered to remain in the forward trench.

173rd Tunnelling Company Royal Engineers had driven two tunnels, 285 and 330 feet long and twenty metres apart, through the blue clay under the saturated surface loam, ending in mine chambers each primed with 2000 lbs of explosives. The bright clay spoil had been carefully bagged and carried away so as not to betray the secret workings. German attempts to mine in this sector had been abandoned due to the waterlogged ground and the 17th Bavarian Reserve Regiment diary states:

> the British offensive came as a surprise on our front. No special preparations had been noticed, and even the presence of the mines driven under the front trenches of the regiment next to us had not been perceived.

1/13 London Regiment (The Kensingtons), a territorial battalion keyed up and anxious to prove their fighting qualities to the regulars of the other battalions in the Brigade, attacked some 300 yards away from the main body, on the extreme left flank of the front. Their attack was well executed and amongst the most successful of the battle.

With just eighty yards of No Man's Land separating them from their German adversaries, amidst thunderous noise and with the ground shaking under a frantic miscellany of explosions as the artillery barrage rained down a mere fifty yards ahead, the Kensingtons waited fearfully for the greatest roar of all – the explosions of the largest mines to date, planned to obliterate eighty yards of the German front and reserve lines. However, the War Diary cryptically records:

> *5 am: Bombardment began. It appeared to lack the intensity of the Neuve Chapelle bombardment. 5.30 am: A battery of 4.7 Howitzers should be bombarding Delangre Farm our chief objective – no shell has struck it as yet.*

On 5 May the Kensingtons had moved from their billets in Laventie to bivouac at Bac St Maur. Until the evening of 8 May the time there was spent in very careful and thorough preparation, specifically training and rehearsing the forthcoming assault planned to follow the mine blasts. On the 6th – 'a most hot and stuffy day' – company officers visited the front to view the terrain, and detailed battle orders were issued by the Adjutant, Lieutenant Cecil Howard.*

*(see appendix 4 - transcript of Battalion Operational Orders No 2. p 185)

On the 8th the CO, Lieutenant-Colonel FG Lewis, attended the final battle briefing at Brigade HQ and, at 5 pm, C Company moved off to the fire trenches. With the onset of darkness, those detailed crept over the breastworks to cut access ways through the guarding wire, whilst others prepared the parapets for rapid deployment. The rest of the battalion paraded and moved off at 10.50 pm, 'with full confidence and in excellent spirits. The battalion ready for action', to join C Company in the front lines. D Company, with B Company behind them, settled to the left, with A Company falling in behind C Company on the right of the 100 yards wide attack front.

At 5.40 am, as the two huge and separate charges were detonated together, the ground in front of them heaved upwards with a deafening roar, drowning even the noise of the bombardment. Earth, debris, and the fragmented bodies of forty eight men of No. 10 Company 16

Heavy artillery being manouvered into position prior to the bombardment.

Firing the mine from Cellar Farm before the Kensingtons go over.

Bavarian Reserve Infantry Regiment and their shattered equipment, spewed high into the air. Above a pall of black smoke the crown of earth hovered momentarily before falling back to earth as shock waves reverberated through the ground.

Charging across the waste ground of No Man's Land in lines of platoon as the debris settled, the assault companies of the Kensingtons took possession of the newly formed ramparts of the mine craters. D Company regrouped, and again hurried forward under intermittent fire to overrun the second and third line trenches and then on to attack the strong point at Delangre Farm. The rapid advance was brought to a halt at a track some fifty yards short of the fortress farm, which contained within its fortifications at least two heavy machine gun emplacements, bristled with rifles, and had remained practically untouched by British howitzers. The company survivors again regrouped, forced possession of a German communication trench, and formed a left facing defensive flank line, then extended their line fifty yards to the south.

C Company, meanwhile, had packed into the crater rim and cautiously pushed to the right along the first and second line German trenches. The defending German infantrymen on the flanks, having been utterly shocked by the devastation caused by the totally unexpected mine explosions, quickly regained composure to reform and pour heavy fire into the ranks of B and A Companies as they crossed No Man's Land to swell the breakthrough.

German field telephone lines to 3rd Battalion 16 Reserve Infantry Regiment HQ at Fromelles had been cut by British shellfire. Informed of the breaches by runner, Brigadier-General Kiefhaber ordered Major von Luneschloss immediately to relocate his 3rd Battalion HQ closer to the front at Turk's Corner (Turkenecke), and ordered 12 Company, plus two platoons from 11 Company, forward from reserve to reinforce

10 Company, which had been seriously depleted by the mine explosions and the sudden follow up attack.

On the right of the Kensingtons the German defenders, swiftly reorganising after the shock, packed a defensive block to halt any further lateral advance by C Company, which had intruded by bombing along the trenches to the right. On arrival, 12 Company 16th Bavarians reinforced the strong barricade formed to stem any further moves to widen the breach beyond the fifty yards already captured to the left of the crater and, with added assistance from 21st Regiment and, in readiness for counter attack, formed a defensive line opposing the Kensingtons newly established forward positions in the communication trench and along the track running north-north west from Delangre Farm.

The rear supply routes by this time were being peppered by unrelenting shellfire and the stretch of No Man's Land supporting troops had to cross was a maelstrom of rifle and machine gun fire. Brigadier-General Lowry Cole on receiving the news of the Kensingtons breakthrough had immediately sent a message of congratulation to Lieutenant Colonel Lewis and, after ordering the 1/1 London Regiment to advance from reserve trenches to support and sustain the attack, he moved up to direct operations from a forward position in the breastworks.

To the rear of the old British front line the four companies of 1/1 London Regiment, which had moved up the previous evening from billets at Bac St Maur, were ordered forward from their positions in assembly trenches south of the Rue Petillon to support the attack. As the British bombardment started at 5 am the answering German batteries dropped high explosive on their assembly trenches. Starting forward at 5.40 am, A Company, with C Company on their right, followed by B Company with D Company on the left and HQ behind, were almost immediately ordered to halt, A Company sheltering in shallow trenches and C Company huddled in the open.

Ordered at 6.10 am to continue the advance in rushes by platoon, on rising, those on the right of the battalion were immediately hit by intense rifle and machine gun fire. Before reaching the Riviere des Laies three officers and 120 men had been lost, although C and D Companies on the left suffered only few casualties.

A, B and D Companies lined the front assembly trenches with C Company and HQ to their rear. Access to the front fire trenches was impossible, being filled with intermixed wounded and milling troops from 2/Royal Berks, 2/Lincolns, and some Devons and Sherwood Foresters. 'The advance was not continued.'

At 6.25 am Brigadier-General Lowry Cole arrived to discover the 1/1 London Regiment had lost the three officers and 120 men even before reaching the breastworks, forward movement was arrested and, with the two lead companies of 2/Lincolns pinned down on the right, and with enemy fire relentless, the situation was critically balanced between being able to consolidate the successful breakthrough and the whole action being overcome and repulsed by counterattack.

He ordered Y and Z companies of 2/Lincolns, which had remained hemmed in behind their parapets, to move via the sap and a shallow communication trench and to advance to the mine craters, from there to work to the right, bombing along the German line to connect with the trenches held by troops of 1/RIR and 2/Rifle Brigade.

However, at the same time as 2/Lincolns, under the command of Captain BJ Thruston, doubled across the final stretch of open ground towards the craters, many men of the Rifle Brigade and the Royal Irish Rifles were spotted hurriedly retreating back over the German breastworks. As brigade staff leapt to order the troops back, German prisoners, running for cover behind the British lines were mistakenly identified as counter attackers and were fired upon from the British trenches. With his staff trying to restore order in the ensuing confusion, Major Dill, the Brigade Major, was badly wounded and, whilst imploring his troops to return immediately to the German front line trench, Brigadier-General Lowry Cole was hit and collapsed mortally wounded.

In the absence of Lieutenant-Colonel Stephens, the most senior of the battalion officers, who was in the German trench with his remaining troops, Major F Fitz G Cox of 2/Lincolns temporarily assumed command of 25 Brigade and Major AER Boxer took over command of 2/Lincolns.

Extensive enquiries after the battle into the retreat incident failed to determine a reason for the unauthorised withdrawal, except that an instruction to 'retire at the double!' had been shouted with great fury and quickly and positively repeated.

2/Royal Berkshire Regt, having moved on 6 May from Laventie to billets at Bac St Maur, east of Sailly, paraded at 11 pm on 8 May then moved forward for three miles in the darkness to assume their positions in the appointed assembly trenches, behind 2/Rifle Brigade and 1/Royal Irish Rifles, in readiness to follow in support as the assault troops attacked. C and D Companies advanced to occupy the front breastwork as the Rifle Brigade went over the top, with A and B Companies following.

Captain Nugent, commanding D Company, records that on his arrival in the front trench many of the Rifle Brigade still waited there, and that the fire trenches in front were filled with men. On looking over the parapet he saw many of those who had already gone over lying pinned down under strafing fire amongst the foot high vegetation. Shortly after, Lieutenants Lipscombe and Cuncliffe lead the first two sections of 15 and 16 platoons over the breastworks, whilst the other two sections prepared to advance and follow without delay. The four leading sections of 13 and 14 platoons, led by Captain Nugent and Lieutenant Day, scrambled over the parapet and rushed forward to occupy the old fire trench and sap which was already overcrowded and milling with men of C Company 2/Rifle Brigade and some Irish Riflemen, who claimed to have been ordered by person unknown to remain there. They were ordered to join forces with the Berkshires and to advance in two rushes. The first was to about the halfway mark and, having regrouped, to then storm forward to occupy the enemy trenches.

Upon dropping after the first rush, men of the Rifle Brigade and Irish Rifles appeared over the German breastworks running and stumbling back shouting 'retire at the double!' When halted and questioned by Captain Nugent a terrified junior NCO earnestly retorted that the order to retire had been given by a 'Captain Dee of the Royal Irish Rifles'.

Captain Nugent ordered his men to crawl back to the fire trench and to remain there until further notice. The old forward fire trench and sap were prepared, as well as the chaotic circumstances would allow in the midst of gunfire and explosions, in readiness for the expected hurried arrival of retiring assault troops and the machine guns were relocated, more securely, behind the breastworks.

Appealing for direction to Major Cox, who by that time had assumed acting command of the brigade, Captain Nugent was ordered immediately to reorganise the men of his regiment behind breastwork and there to await further instructions.

Only the first two sections of B Company, organised in four lines to follow behind D Company, had crossed over the parapet. The rest remained behind the breast works, according to Second Lieutenants Lindley and Lewis, having been ordered to stay there by Lieutenant Aldworth.

Captain C Nugent, in his appendix to the Battalion War Diary; recounts statements concerning the unscheduled withdrawals:.

Sergeant Matthews in charge of the leading platoon wrote in his statement that his men became mixed with men of the Rifle Brigade who remained in the front breastwork and who, by an officer, were being urged by shouted orders to get over the parapet. On dropping over the parapet and advancing at the double he was knocked over and buried under a wall of earth lifted by a shell explosion and, by the time he had been pulled out and recovered, men of the Rifle Brigade with some collected additions from the 2/Berkshires were running back through his company shouting, 'retire at the double'. On demanding to know the whereabouts of the company officers he was informed they were all dead. Together with four NCOs and 47 men he returned to the breastworks, where he was ordered to regroup his troops and wait in readiness to move under the command of Lieutenant Hawkins to reinforce the front line. The move did not take place.

Sergeant Wilder, 10 Platoon, C Company, on the right flank of the battalion attack, stated that from his position leading the second line he saw Lieutenant Watson, who was leading the first line, shot and fall back dead. Under fire, his own platoon moved amongst and went forward with the first line, deviating slightly to the right towards the ruins of a red house beyond the German trench, the sight line of their advance. After passing through a group of several riflemen prostrate in the wheat field, a message by mouth from the rear ordered, 'From the Brigade Commander, no further advance' and, after a few minutes a second order, 'Advance to the first German trench'. About to rise and advance he saw what he describes as a fairly strong group of men hurrying back from the German trench shouting, 'retire at the double!' As the group approached he ordered them to halt, take cover, and remain where they were. Unable to discover the source of the order to retire, Sergeant Wilder returned to Company HQ, where he was told to bring back his men to join Sergeant Matthews and his men in the breastwork and to reorganise.

Such was the confusion on the battlefield that Captain MacGregor, leading the first A Company troops following behind C Company, actually passed through C Company and carrying some men of that company forward with his platoons, actually reached the German trench before being hit and incapacitated by his wounds. Other A Company platoons failed to reach the German lines, Second Lieutenant Druitt was killed and Second Lieutenant West severely wounded. Captain MacGregor was never seen again.

At about 11.15 am the regrouped 2/Royal Berkshires, now commanded by Captain Nugent, were instructed, by message brought from the Brigade Major by Lieutenant Hawkins, to file to the left and, via sap and communication trench, thence to crawl man by man across the open ground to reinforce troops in the German breastworks.

The decisive repulse of the 24 Brigade attack on the British right flank of the northern prong of the pincer movement had enabled the German commander quickly to re-deploy troops to counteract the developing danger on his right flank - the British left.

Troops were sent forward from the supporting 5/16th Bavarians to augment the German strength in the Rouge Bancs area, and a third company deployed to check the 2/Rifle Brigade advance. The troops remaining in the German front line flanking the British advance fought to hold their positions whilst all available firepower was concentrated on preventing any forward flow of support, and to contain the British troops who had broken through. With support failing to appear, the two companies of 2/Rifle Brigade, under machine gun fire from both flanks and rear, and in danger of being marooned by counter attack, fell back as best they could to the German front line trenches to defend the 400 yards wide breach.

On leaving the mine craters the men of 2/Lincolns, under Captain Thruston, who had been ordered forward by Brigadier-General Lowry Cole, lost direction in a maze of trenches and became engaged in fierce hand to hand fighting. Second Lieutenant EO Black, commanding the

2/Lincolnshires in the mine crater, 9 May 1915.

IWM Q50418

bomb and block party detailed to clear the German front trench westwards, was hit and wounded soon after the start, and with lateral progress delayed, and many casualties being suffered, the position was retrieved by the singular action of acting Corporal CR Sharpe. One of the first to engage the enemy, he lead his party to bomb and clear fifty yards along the German trench until all bombs were expended; he alone remained then, when joined by four others from the regiment with extra bombs, he continued his attack, clearing about another 200 yards of trench before his bomb supply became again exhausted. Corporal Sharpe was awarded the Victoria Cross. He survived the war, rising to the rank of CSM. His medal is displayed in the Museum of Lincolnshire Life, Lincoln.

A seconded bombing section from 2/Scottish Rifles was ordered to bomb eastwards from the crater, but all efforts to dislodge the defenders on that left flank were to no avail. All were under extreme and unceasing machine gun fire from both front, left and right, and the 2/Lincolns' War Diary records:

> 9.00 am; Men sent over to establish defence of cleared trenches suffered many casualties. Only few arrived.

Five heavy machine guns captured by Captain Thruston's 2/Lincolns were turned in concentrated fire onto two German machine posts, whose guns were strafing from beyond the craters, and 'quickly silenced them'. 2/Lincolns consolidated and tenuously held the 300 yards of captured trench but were unable to extend the lateral advance to their right to connect with Lieutenant-Colonel Stephens's 2/Rifle Brigade.

The intermixed 2/Rifle Brigade and 1/Royal Irish Riflemen, cut off in the trench system they had captured to the right of the Sailly –

Fromelles road, would hold position throughout the day in spite of constant counter attacks.

A short artillery barrage was ordered onto the stretch of German held trench connecting that held by the Kensingtons/Lincolns to that in the possession of RIR/Rifle Brigade. The survivors of the two lead companies 2/Lincolns, who had been pinned down in front of their own parapets, were ordered to storm the stretch of battered trench frontally. The attack withered and died almost immediately under a renewed onslaught from the German troops resolutely defending their broken lines in spite of all British efforts to subdue their resolve.

At about four o'clock in the afternoon Captain Thruston received an order to withdraw, but mass movement of troops before dark would have meant almost certain death. Having no bombs or serviceable machine guns remaining, the withdrawal was precipitated when, at about 8 pm, bomb and rush attacks on their positions from both flanks started in earnest. Second Lieutenant Black disappeared during the return journey and was not seen again. During the short period of desperate close fighting which developed as the Bavarians fought to repossess the trench and the Lincolns made haste to exit, a particular instance of bravery occurred. Private W. Cowling held up a party of enemy troops whilst a considerable number of his colleagues scrambled to escape. Frantically scrapping hand to hand with rifle and bayonet he disabled several German soldiers before the weapons were wrested from his grasp. He then managed to twist away from capture and scuttle away. He was awarded the Distinguished Conduct Medal in recognition of his selfless action.

The effect of the rapid German application of their defensive tactics

2/Scottish Rifles 6 May 1915, in reserve behind La Cordonnerie Farm.

to prevent replenishment and, wherever possible, immediately to counterattack any intrusion, is encapsulated by an entry in the Kensingtons' War Diary:

> *6.45 am There was no sign of any British troops on our right or behind us. Our right flank was completely in the air and the whole line was suffering from fire from Delangre Farm. Our machine gun on the right was disabled...The machine guns of the West Riding Division were firing into us.*
>
> *7.00 am The supply of bombs was running short and a message was sent to Brigade Headquarters for reinforcements and bombs.*

Dogged fighting to hold positions continued with the ammunition becoming steadily depleted to uncomfortably low levels.

At 9.05 am from Brigade to Battalion HQ, '2nd Scottish Rifles moving to support you. You have done splendidly'.

The arrival, timed at 9.10 am, of an officer and two bombers of 2/Scottish Rifles 'with a small supply of bombs', obviously did not impress the CO; his message, timed at 10.45 am to Brigade HQ, reads,

> *No signs of Scottish Rifles or ammunition. Please expedite both. Position is unchanged but casualties increasing. Should Germans attack before support comes fear I cannot hold on.*

At about 10 am Lieutenant Sewell, who had been reported hit and disabled at 7.30 am and had lain wounded in Battalion HQ since 8.45 am, died of his injuries. With Captain Barnett mortally wounded, Second Lieutenant Laurie killed and Second Lieutenant Stern severely wounded, the early elation of the Kensingtons success was turning into desperation. Starting at about 10.30 am, for about an hour, a signaller tried repeatedly to establish direct communication with the British in their breastworks from a captured German sap, but his efforts went unheeded.

At 11.30 am: 'Last grenade used. Ammunition very short'.

For the next four hours the Kensingtons, tenuously stretched from the mine craters to their positions near Delangre Farm, fought against increasing pressure from both flanks as the reorganised adversaries of 12 Company 16th Bavarians were joined by troops from 21st Regiment with extra bombing parties.

With bombs and trench mortar the German infantrymen, commanded by Lieutenant Schmitt, overcame blocks in trenches to the right of the craters and the resulting enfilade fire caused very heavy casualties. Although frantic resistance by the Kensingtons stemmed a complete breakthrough, they were gradually pushed back towards the craters. Many isolated troops, disorientated and lost, became surrounded and were killed or surrendered and spent the rest of the war as prisoners in Germany.

Sometime before one o' clock five men of the 2/Royal Berkshires reached the craters with bandoliers of ammunition, but without substantial reinforcements the situation had by then become quite untenable. Heavy German pressure from the south of the line forced more troops back to the craters as fire strafed their scant cover.

At 2 pm three companies of 1/Bavarians left Fournes to march up to the forward assembly point north west of Fromelles. On arrival, No 2 Company was detailed to advance at the double to recapture the area to the west of Delangre Farm, where other isolated groups of Kensingtons were still fighting. Unable to move, nearly all of the latter were killed, and only two of those who managed to avoid capture managed to reach their own lines.

The official order to retire to the British breastworks, timed at 2.45 pm, was received by Battalion HQ from Brigadier-General Pinney, temporarily commanding the brigade, although relaying the order and instructing the scattered troops was nigh on impossible and any return crossing of No Man's Land remained extremely dangerous.

Timed at 3.55 pm a final message back to Brigade HQ says:

...the remnants of the Battalion estimated at about 50 strong are in process of rendez–vous in the redoubts near Cellar Farm. A few more are in the crater and may be able to get out.

In fact 55 men managed to get back across No Man's Land to reach Cellar Farm and, throughout the late afternoon and evening, others, in small ragged groups or singly, crawled back to join the survivors in the craters. For his part in the action at Delangre Farm Captain Kimber was awarded the Military Cross. In a letter to his parents he wrote:

We crawled for hours above our waists in the mud and foul water of the German trenches, isolated and cut off by an enemy we could not see, but who was steadily reducing our numbers by very excellent sniping. We were four subalterns in charge of thirty to forty men. Two of the officers were killed. The other man and myself determined to wait until darkness and then try to get through the German lines to our own. It was a risk, but everything was a risk that day.

With the counter attacks by the strengthened Bavarians against the ill supplied Kensingtons increasing in momentum, and with the plan that the 7th Division was to attack afresh the following morning, the order to withdraw back to the original British line was issued. During the cover of darkness the few remaining men of the Kensingtons and Royal Berkshires, defeated, exhausted and hungry, clambered back over the British breastworks.

Second Lieutenant Robertson with two men stumbled back in at 1.45 am and later stragglers dribbled across, having sneaked through the re-occupied German line, the last not arriving until about 3 am. Hundreds of wounded men, lying exposed in the mud, needed to be recovered by stretcher parties as the final gallant action after the totally fruitless assaults.

Only four of the seventeen officers of the Kensingtons involved in the morning assault survived the day unscathed. Eight were killed, four wounded and one was posted as missing.

Continually shelled, the remains of the battalion withdrew at 1 am on 10th May to bivouac off the Fleurbaix road.

A bland statement in their War Diary records that,

> *About 30 Germans were captured, four of whom were taken*
> *by the Colonel in a dugout. Hardly ten reached the British lines.*

The reason for their demise is not recorded.

The final 1/13 London Regt casualty list shows that out of twenty one officers and 602 other ranks, only eight officers and 169 men came through physically unhurt.

On 13th May Major-General Davies visited the battalion to congratulate all on their outstanding efforts. Nine officers had been killed, and four wounded. Of other ranks eighty two died, 180 wounded, fifty three were recorded as wounded and missing and 118 remained unaccounted for.

1/1 London Battalion remained in their forward positions under shellfire throughout the day until withdrawn to billets at Bac St Maur at 9 pm. Roll-call revealed Captain SMD Mouat and Lieutenant RGC Bowen were dead, Lieutenant J Seaverns had died of wounds and Captain AA Lyle and Lieutenant HJ Boyton were wounded. Other rank casualties totalled thirty two killed, 149 wounded and thirteen missing.

2/Lincolns were withdrawn from the forward reserve trenches at 11 pm, reaching billets at Bac St Maur at 2 am on 10 May 1915. The roll call records twenty eight dead, seventy seven missing and 172 wounded. Lieutenant HM Goldsmith, Second Lieutenant RDM Nisbet, Second Lieutenant GF Ayres (3/Dorsets) and Second Lieutenant HR Buddon (3/Dorsets), had been killed, Second Lieutenant EO Black was missing presumed dead, and Second Lieutenant HGF Clifford, Second

Intent on the map in the ruins of La Cordonnerie (Cellar) Farm.

IWM Q56180

Lieutenant PH Parker and Lieutenant EH Nind (3/Dorsets) wounded.

The Germans in the line had also suffered extensive casualties from the heavy and continuing bombardment and the assaults, but lessons from the earlier attack at Neuve Chapelle had been well learned. With their greatly improved defences and many heavy machine guns strategically deployed overlooking the British positions, although inferior in number, the German defenders had successfully repelled the bulk of the attacks against their positions. Contain and counter attack as quickly as possible was the strategy repeatedly executed with great efficiency, regardless of the confusion of battle.

Major-General FJ Davies, in his HQ on the Rue de Bacquerot just south west of Fleurbaix, had waited impatiently for information regarding 24 and 25 Brigade attacks. At about 7.45 am he was advised not only of the total failure of the 24 Brigade attack, but also that Brigadier-General Lowry Cole was dead. His General Staff Officer, Colonel WF Anderson, had been sent at once to instruct Brigadier-General Pinney, commanding the reserve 23 Brigade, to assume command of all the troops in the sector east of the Sailly – Fromelles road, and to brief him as to the situation at the front.

After struggling through inadequate communication trenches smashed by continually exploding shells and overloaded with stretcher-bearers and mud bespattered wounded, he found the conditions around the breastworks and trenches were chaotic and units totally confused. The whole front, a quagmire pitmarked with waterfilled craters, was strewn with bodies, littered with a confusion of torn equipment and stores, the wounded and bleeding crying out for assistance and small

115

groups of ragged and mud smattered soldiers, disorientated and leaderless, were seeking any shelter available. Brigadier-General Pinney quickly assessed the unsavoury situation and reported back to General Davies that:

> *A section of enemy trench east of the Sailly – Fromelles road had been captured and was held by 2/Rifle Brigade and 1/Royal Irish Rifles*
>
> *A remnant of two companies 2/Lincolnshire Regt held a section of the same trench to their left.*
>
> *A detachment of 1/13 London Regiment held the mine craters some distance again to their left.*
>
> *All were subjected to continual bombardment and were being strafed by the enemy from positions within and behind the sections of trench between the short British held segments.*

General Rawlinson, already advised that, with the exception of the small intrusion by 2/Northants, the 24 Brigade attack had failed entirely, was painfully aware that after three hours of very costly fighting the offensive was at a standstill.

In the excellent book *1915: The Death of Innocence,* by Lyn MacDonald, an account of the overwhelming difficulties in dealing with the extraordinary flow of wounded is recalled by Private L. Mitchell, who worked in the 24th Field Ambulance main dressing station west of Petillon crossroads. He states that for three days without a break the wounded were tended as they arrived and still sixty or seventy stretcher cases lay outside awaiting dressing. When his superior, a Medical Corps Major collapsed exhausted, he had personally to assume responsibility for administering anaesthetics to amputees. Splints and dressings were applied to the very large proportion of the casualties who were bullet wounded in the lower limbs. Ambulance vehicles were filled continually and sent back to the Casualty Clearing Stations.

Twice he had to inject extra morphia into soldiers with impossible wounds, one man with,

> *no eyes, no nose, no chin, no mouth – and still alive, another man with a piece of steel, a big chunk of shell, sticking out of his breastbone and sticking out of his back. He also had an arm smashed up and very severe head wounds – and he was still alive. The extra morphia was not administered off my own bat, The Officer tells you to do it and you do it – but you don't forget! When I got home after the war I sometimes used to have a nightmare and wake up in the night thinking my arms were covered with blood, It wore off eventually.*

First Aid for the walking wounded.

I remember very clearly my father still being haunted by similar nightmares fifty years after the horrific events.

The 7th Division, commanded by Major-General H de la P Gough, was in reserve, ready to push forward when the 8th Division had secured their objectives.

Brigadier-General STB Lawford detailed 2/Royal West Surrey Regt (Queen's) and 2/Royal Warwicks to lead his 22 Brigade, and on 8 May they had marched from Estaires via La Gorgue to assume positions in reserve trenches west of Petillon. As the 8th Division attack got under way the battalions moved up to forward support trenches behind the Rue de Petillon, some 400 to 500 yards behind the front line. As attacks failed there they stayed throughout the day. The War Diary of the 2/Queen's shows casualties of one other rank killed and thirteen wounded by shellfire, and the Medical Officer Lieutenant EH Griffin, as wounded.

On the evening of 9 May the 7th Division troops started the march back to billets around Essars – a distance of some twelve miles. Captain Haddon, D Company 2/Queen's, remained, temporarily drafted to the

8th Division to assist in reorganising and evacuating the wounded.

To the south the French Army, under the command of General Petain, had opened their attack after an intensive and sustained bombardment of the German lines and support areas. The infantry advanced across a six kilometres wide breach of the German defences and pushed forward more than three kilometres into the high ground of Vimy Ridge. With reserves and the supporting field artillery becoming increasingly distant behind the rapid advance the opportunity presented by the spectacular breakthrough could not be fully exploited. The Germans regrouped and after close and determined fighting over the following days the French secured Carency and Ablain St.Nazaire near the heights of Notre Dame de Lorette, but the momentum of the advance was stemmed.

Before the 10 am opening of the successful French advance on the morning of 9 May 1915 the British attack fronts were in total disarray. The initial attacks had been peremptorily repulsed, the attacking battalions had suffered extreme casualties and those remaining were rendered ineffective by accurate fire from the excellent German defences. Although the Germans had suffered much damage and many casualties, their firepower remained extremely effective. The British lines, rear positions and routes to the front, were all under continual artillery barrage. The hurriedly built British breastworks and the surrounding areas were a complete mess, regrouping the disjointed remnants of battalions with insufficient officers was proving extremely difficult, access from rear areas was perilous and, with front line communications almost non existent, any attempt to launch a new attack at short notice was doomed to failure.

General Haig, some distance removed from the chaos of the battlefield, would not or could not accept the news of failures received at Army HQ, first from divisional and then confirmed by his corps commanders. His army, much superior in number and executing an operation so meticulously planned, could not have failed so ignominiously. Informed during the morning that the French Tenth Army to the south had broken through and forced back the German line, spurred his determination to succeed. His duty, and a prime object of the operation, was to maintain pressure on the German front in his zone, thereby to assist the French in exploiting to the full their attack. Another determined push against what must now be much damaged and crippled German defences would surely result in a collapse of enemy resistance, allowing his reserve divisions to pour across and seize the ridge.

As the extent of the failure and the isolation of those who occupied parts of the German trenches became known, and with full knowledge that the Indian and 1st Division attacks had failed, Haig twice ordered Rawlinson, first at 8.45 am, repeated at 11.45 am, to, 'press the attack vigorously and without delay on Rouges Bancs'.

The impatient General Haig, who was growing more apprehensive as time passed, stressed to his commanders the need to attack again. Brigadier-Generals Oxley, of 24 Brigade, and Pinney, temporarily commanding 25 Brigade, answered with due deference to Major-General Davies, their 8th Division Commander, that their lead battalions were mostly spread around in No Man's Land and a renewal of hostile action would not be possible for some hours. The Kensingtons, still holding their ground around the mine craters in spite of increasing pressure, were reinforced by 200 men of 2/Royal Berkshires mustered from the troops in the wrecked breastworks. Under the command of Captain C Nugent they crawled in single file along the shallow shell pocked communication trench to the craters with a continual hail of bullets whistling just above their heads, bringing with them supplies of critically needed ammunition and bombs. The number of battle fit troops available was totally inadequate to mount any frontal assault on the scale demanded by the generals.

The confusion and destruction along the whole front was appreciated at this stage neither by Rawlinson nor by Haig from their HQ positions, necessarily well distanced behind the lines and without efficient communication connections. Haig, in particular, so anxious for success, would not accept failure and, without proper attention to dwindling reserves of ammunition and troops, was again driven to demand a repeat of the ineffective tactics of the opening assault at whatever the cost.

Under repeated pressure from Haig, Rawlinson decided that, because the whereabouts of his troops in those stretches of trench occupied since the first assault was not precisely known, his attack would have to be against the 400 yards of German trench west of the Sailly – Fromelles road, against which 2/East Lancs and 1/Sherwood Foresters attack had earlier crumpled.

As the position of the troops in the German trenches was not clearly defined, another barrage was ordered to concentrate on 500 yards of trench to the south of Fromelles road – the stretch of German trench between the road and the section occupied by the small party of 2/Northants.

With Brigadier-General Pinney having sent the last of his available troops – the 200 2/Royal Berkshires – to reinforce the Kensingtons, Brigadier General Oxley, notwithstanding his repeated opinion that the attack could not succeed, was instructed by General Davies to attack 'with what men you can muster'. He ordered forward his reserve battalions, 1/Worcestershires under Lieutenant-Colonel Grogan, and 1/5 Black Watch, with instructions to be prepared and ready to attack at 1.30 pm. 2/Queen's, from 7th Division, commanded by Major HR Bottomley, were to support, and 2/Middlesex and 1/7 Middlesex of 23 Brigade, who had been holding the line for the twelve days prior to the battle, were to act as the reserve battalions.

At 12.50 pm the artillery opened fire on the 400 yards of German trench again, breaking the assembled battalions and inflicting many casualties with scattered 'shorts'. The German artillery, accurately sighted on the British front trenches, earnestly opened up with an answering barrage. The unprotected battalions suffered crippling losses before they could even attempt to attack, and Lieutenant-Colonel Grogan, certain of the futility of trying to cross against the undamaged German defences prickling with heavy machine guns, on his own volition cancelled the 24 Brigade attack. 1/Worcesters had lost 235 men and 1/5 Black Watch another 146 men without even crossing their own breastworks.

Just before 2 pm, as he was finishing his lunch in the Indian Corps Mess, General Haig received the news by despatch rider that 25 Brigade had been too disabled to attack, and that the 24 Brigade assault had been aborted. His scribbled retort, returned to Rawlinson by the same despatch rider, stated that the 24 and 25 Brigades attacks had been totally unsatisfactory and that an additional brigade from General Gough's 7th Division would be made available forthwith.

Major-General Gough, unable to obtain clarification of the situation on the 8th Division attack front, either from Rawlinson's Corps HQ at Laventie or from the Divisional HQ at Rue de Baquerot, decided to visit the front personally. On arrival he consulted with Brigadier-General Oxley in his scantily protected forward Brigade HQ and, after a quick but incisive inspection of the battleground in chaos, he hurried back to his HQ to discover the message, which had been received during his absence, ordering him to place his 21 Brigade at the disposal of General Rawlinson.

His call by field telephone to Rawlinson described in very stark terms the situation which existed at the front, and furthermore strongly emphasised that any further attempts at assault at the present time would be nothing more than pointless sacrifice.

By the time Haig arrived back at his own HQ the information had been received from the much respected Major-General Gough

2/Royal Scots Fusiliers in forward trench – La Boutillerie, Spring 1915.

repeating that any further daylight action would be doomed to bloody and wasteful failure and that the use of 21 Brigade or any other would, in his opinion, be totally pointless.

General Haig, knowing that failure of the northern pincer of his plan would fatally flaw the offensive, but not yet ready to accept defeat, decided that renewed aggression on the southern pincer front was necessary to achieve the objectives there and to give time to reorganise and rekindle the offensive in the north.

Meanwhile, on the northern pincer front, Brigadier-Generals Pinney and Oxley and their brigades were at this time still very much involved in the continuing struggle. Under unremitting shellfire the hectic work of repairing wrecked trenches and breastworks continued. Gathering, treating, and evacuating the hundreds of wounded, reorganising the intermixed and tattered battalions, as well as the deep mud and shell pocked mess permitted, and trying to supply and service those stranded and involved in the tenuous hold on the short stretches of trench captured during the first wave of the assault, all surrounded by the never ending crackle and spit of deadly small arms fire, was a monumental task.

On the northern front of the pincer movement, the small but untenable British gains of the morning were lost and the German defenders regained possession of the whole of their original line.

The 7th Division was ordered to replace the 8th Division in readiness for another full scale attack the following morning.

Chapter Four

AFTERNOON ATTACK
from the Rue du Bois (Southern Front)

The order from General Haig to attack again on the southern front was, after delays due to the logistical problems of troop assembly and reorganisation in extremely difficult conditions, rescheduled to start at 4 pm following another forty minutes bombardment of the German front line positions.

On the Indian Corps front Lieutenant-General Willcocks ordered the ravaged Dehra Dun Brigade to withdraw, leaving many still wounded and stranded in No Man's Land, to be replaced by the Bareilly Brigade, commanded by Brigadier-General Southey.

Major-General Haking, commanding 1st Division, ordered the two reserve battalions of his 3 Brigade, with two battalions borrowed from 1 Brigade, to carry out this repeat attack against the same heavily fortified breastworks and over the same ground as the earlier fiasco.

The German losses of about 400 men of the 55th Regiment in the morning fighting had been quickly replenished by the arrival of three support companies, and the number of German troops in the front line was in fact, as indicated by RFC Intelligence reports, higher than during the morning assaults. Although the divisional artillery had maintained constant fire on the German forward positions throughout the morning, their defensive strength was undiminished. Howitzer shells being in very short supply, the bulk of the afternoon bombardment was effected using 18pdr HE shells – ineffective in damaging the earthwork parapets. Some damage to the German breastworks was, however, reported to the right of the line, and in several places barbed wire obstacles had been torn.

A. 1st DIVISION. Afternoon attack.
At 12.15 hours Brigadier-General Thesiger had informed Major-

The southern attack front viewed from the German front trench line.

1st DIVISION FRONT

1ST (GUARDS) BRIGADE
1/LOYAL NORTH LANCS 1/5 SUSSEX

1/BLACK WATCH

General Haking that his 2 Brigade was so depleted as to be incapable of mounting an effective afternoon assault. 1 (Guards) Brigade was ordered up from reserve to replace 2 Brigade.

To the left of the Cinder Track, 1/South Wales Borderers and 1/Gloucesters of 3 Brigade, with 1/Camerons and 1/Black Watch of 1st (Guards) Brigade to the right, would lead the assault. 1/Loyal North Lancs and 1/9 King's (Liverpool), having been held back in 2 Brigade divisional reserve, would follow up in support. Major-General Horne assured Major-General Haking that his re-organised 2nd Division would be ready to advance through the 1st Division on breakthrough.

1/Black Watch, with a complement of 24 officers and 981 other ranks, had been alternating with 1/Camerons holding the front line from Chocolat Menier Corner to the Cinder Track prior to the battle. On 7 May orders advising that the battalion would be in active reserve for the forthcoming attack were received.

Starting at 7.55 am on 9 May, A, B and D Companies had moved forward to occupy forward reserve trenches. C Company stayed in second line breastworks with two companies of 1/Coldstream Guards. The other two companies of 1/Coldstream Guards, and 1/Scots Guards, moved behind them to occupy the second line breastworks with 1/14 London (London Scottish) in the third line, ready to repulse any counter attacks or to move forward to consolidate and secure gains. To replace casualties sustained by artillery fire in the forward trenches, C Company had been ordered to move forward at about 10 am.

At 11.05 orders were received that the battalion would lead an assault starting at 12.40 after a forty minute barrage, the last fifteen minutes of which would be intensive.

At 11.45 am the start was delayed until 2.40 pm, and at 12.45 pm again delayed until 4 pm. At 2.20 pm the commanding officer lead his company commanders forward to survey the ground and determine the direction and objectives for each company, and at 3 pm packs were stacked ready for the assault. The battalion was to capture the German front line between R2 and R6, then to occupy the enemy second line.

In an article written in 1932 Linton Andrews (a journalist and then editor of *The Leeds Mercury*) repeated from notes he made timed at 3.30 p.m. whilst waiting in the front trench ready to go forward.

> *Under bombardment. Nerve-racking medley of roar and clatter. We are lying as low as possible. From the bottom of the trench I can see white puffs (shrapnel in the sky) also dense yellow-brown clouds where German high-explosive shells strike near our trench. Overhead aeroplanes are like filmy silver-grey moths against the glorious sky. Rushing winds accompany the whooshing and whooping and whistling of the shells, and earth continually topples over into the trenches. Have just been struck by a piece of shell – only a scratch on my right hand.*

Ordered into the assault trench he continued;

> *We saw now why our progress has been checked. A narrow trench was crowded with dead, dying, and ammunition. Each of us had to take a box of ammunition and push on to the front trench. Here, too, we were shelled, though not as vigorously as before. Evidently Jerry knew all about our crammed communication trenches, and was sowing death where it would reap the biggest harvest.*

With A Company on the right of their front and D Company the left, supported by B Company and C Company, the troops awaited the order to rapid advance. Two machine guns moved left to align on a gap blown in the enemy breastwork through which a communication trench could be sighted. At 3.37 pm, just before the bombardment started, the machine guns opened fire on the trench and, in spite of the counter barrage answering the fire, continued intermittently throughout the action.

The bombardment of the German trench system in front of the 1/Black Watch seemed to have been more effective than the morning effort, gaps in the defensive barbed wire and damage to the breastworks were clearly visible.

Twenty minutes into the artillery bombardment Major E Craig Brown, commanding officer of 1/Camerons, who were to attack on the left of 1/Black Watch, informed Brigadier-General Lowther, at 1st Brigade HQ, by field telephone, that his battalion would not be on station in readiness for the 4 pm start. This confirmed his earlier warnings, the battalion having been repeatedly delayed during the

The Southern attack front viewed from the German front trench line.

1st DIVISION FRONT

1/CAMERONS

3 BRIGADE
1/4 ROYAL WELSH FUSILIERS
1/GLOUCESTERS

LACK WATCH → 1/NORTHANTS

Viewed from Princes Road to Port Arthur, the British Front Line turned parallel to Princes Road. The 1/Northants in the dawn attack and the 1/Black Watch in the afternoon attacked from left to right of this view.

hindered move up from reserve. He was ordered to attack immediately upon arrival.

The relayed message was received by 1/Black Watch HQ at 3.50 pm and, at 3.55 pm, Brigade HQ advised 1/Black Watch to assault as ordered, 1/Camerons would follow when ready.

With the Camerons absent, at 3.57 pm, just before the barrage lifted, A and D Companies 1/Black Watch crossed the parapet, leapt from the breastworks, formed up, and kilted and inspired by the defiant plaint of accompanying bagpipes, hurried forward at the double to cross the torn and shell holed mess that was No Man's Land stretching out before them. After an interval of eighty yards the first two platoons of B and C Companies followed and at the same time the first two platoons of 1/Camerons came over to their left, followed shortly thereafter by a further two platoons.

Men of the Sussex Regiment, who had lain trapped throughout the day, stirred by the pipes, rose to join the Royal Highlanders as they surged past. The diminishing refrains of bagpipes were sustained until hundred yards short of the enemy trench, except for those of Lance Corporal Stewart who, although injured, piped his defiance right up to the German lines. He was subsequently awarded the Distinguished Conduct Medal.

MEERUT DIVISION
BAREILLY BRIGADE
58TH VAUGHANS RIFLES

JTH WALES
RDERERS   2/BLACK WATCH   1 COY 1/4 BLACK WATCH   41ST DOGRAS

On the right Second Lieutenant Lyles' platoon reached a gap in the wire at 3.59 pm having crossed 300 yards of debris and hole strewn waste in a little over two minutes. Major FMB Robertson, who joined the battalion only on the day before the battle, was hit by bullets just fifty yards short of the enemy line but, although heavy shellfire repeatedly scarred the ground, casualties amongst the men were surprisingly light at this stage. Corporal John Ripley stood exposed on the enemy parapet, directing men to one gap in the torn wire, whilst another narrow gap was temporarily blocked by milling soldiers tearing their way through. B Company were strafed and the second and third waves stopped by the increasingly concentrated fire, but the leading platoons of A Company and D Company with C Company platoons following up, fought their way into the German front lines, cleared a stretch of trench and pursued with bombs Germans retreating along their communication trench. Second Lieutenant Sotheby and his platoon sought unsuccessfully to find a way through on the extreme right flank and were raked by machine gun fire. The advanced platoons reached the German support trench, established blocks, and awaited the arrival of their supporting colleagues but German bombers, quickly counter attacking along parallel communication trenches, fought determinedly to cut off the leading Royal Highlanders.

The second and third platoons of A Company, joined by the first platoon of B Company, under Second Lieutenant Wallace, found a way through and crowded over the damaged enemy parapet. On the right the platoon lead by Lieutenant Lyle pushed on to reach the second trench where blocks were established both in that trench and in a communication trench running off to the right but, with only three bombs with them, the platoon was soon caught by counter attack. Isolated and under siege all were eventually overcome by persistent bomb and grenade attacks.

Second Lieutenant Wanless's platoon and Second Lieutenant Wallace's platoons secured their flanks in the front enemy trench whilst the signaller by flag managed only 'Try and' of a message calling for machine gun fire on the flanks, before being struck down by rifle fire.

On the right of D Company, the platoon lead by Second Lieutenant Shand came through the wire to find two machine guns situated directly above them which apparently were unable to depress their line of fire sufficiently to hit such close targets. Private Morrison disabled one of the guns with a shot into the lock mechanism, but Lieutenant Shand and a small party of men were killed whilst trying to silence the other, and Sergeant Oram assumed charge. To the left of Sergeant Oram's men,

Second Lieutenant Gray was struck by a bullet from the second line as he crossed the front parapet. On the extreme left Lieutenant Scott and two platoons of C Company broke through the German front line and pressed on towards the second. They were not seen again.

Supporting platoons of 1/Black Watch had been torn to pieces by the resurgence of concentrated machine gun and rifle fire before reaching halfway across No Man's Land, by then also under intense counter bombardment from the German 43rd Field Artillery and two batteries of 7th Foot Artillery Regiment.

Intense Machine gun fire had also stopped the advance of 1/Camerons on the left, leaving the left flank exposed. However, German front line soldiers escaping down a communications trench on the left, ran into reinforcements coming forward, the ensuing confusion presenting an easy target for assaulting riflemen and many were killed. Quickly regrouping, the escapees worked back, bombing the line.

Private Spink signalled by flag a message from Second Lieutenant Wanless wanting machine gun fire to be directed at both flanks, and requesting urgent support.

4.06 pm a message to Brigade HQ, copied to the OC 1/Camerons, stated that first objectives had been accomplished and that support was urgently needed.

4.19 pm Brigade HQ answered that two companies of 1/Loyal North Lancs were to support at once with signallers and machine guns and, another at 4.25 pm said that two more companies would follow at once. Meanwhile timed at

4.10 pm another message back from CO 1/Black Watch stated, 'Send support quickly. A battalion at once', and at 4.26 pm, 'Tell machine guns to watch our flanks.'

4.30 pm 1/Loyal North Lancs reported to 1 Brigade that, 'first two companies almost ready to go forward'.

4.32 pm Message from 2 Brigade HQ to 1/Loyal North Lancs, 'Cancel order to support assault and remain in fire trench'.

4.36 pm Message from 1 Brigade to 1/Camerons, 'You have to stand fast'.

4.42 pm 1 Brigade to 1/Black Watch, 'Attacking troops are to be withdrawn under cover of artillery fire to breastworks'.

Second Lieutenant Wanless gave the order for men to retire, which was passed down the line. The men retired under fire and by 5.15pm were withdrawn to the British second line from where they moved by platoon down the Rue de Bois to Le Touret and on to billets at Hinges.

The War Diary records, 'Wind NE, Weather Very fine'.

Roll call revealed that the battalion had incurred casualties of fourteen officers and 461 men. Lieutenant WHC Edwards had been killed. Posted wounded and missing were; Second Lieutenants A Wanless, A Shand, A Gray, and J Wallace; wounded were Major FJB Robertson, Captain W Green, Second Lieutenant TF Murdoch, Lieutenant JEM Richard and Second Lieutenant JBS Haldane, and missing were; Second Lieutenants JG Scott, JB Lyle, G Bone and H West. Other rank losses were listed as 61 dead, 241 wounded, six wounded and missing, and 153 missing. The battalion fighting strength had been reduced to eight officers and 354 other ranks.

Corporal John Ripley, 1/Black Watch, was awarded the Victoria Cross. He was the first man of the battalion to reach the enemy parapet where, under extreme fire, he directed the troops following through a gap in the wire entanglement. He then lead his section through to the second enemy trench and, with eight others, blocked the flanks and established a position which they held until, with severe head injuries, he was the last to fall. 47 years of age at the time, he survived the war, achieving the rank of sergeant.

On 11 May, in divisional reserve at Hinges, HRH Prince of Wales visited the battalion and Major-General Haking visited to convey personally 'congratulations to the battalion on the gallant example on 9th' from Lieutenant-General Sir CC Munro, GOC I Corps and General Sir Douglas Haig, Commander First Army. Two days later the Prince of Wales again visited, accompanied by Lieutenant-General Munro, the latter of whom addressed the troops and again expressed his congratulations on their 'fine behaviour'.

1/Camerons, bivouaced on a farm and orchard 300 yards west of Windy Corner in divisional reserve, awaited attack orders. Ordered to follow 3 Brigade and to press through the attack, the battalion moved up into reserve trenches and at 8 am on 9 May were advised that the 3 Brigade attack had failed and they were to relieve three companies of 2/Welsh in the front trenches. A, C and D Companies, with B Company in the second line, completed their relocation at 10.15 am. At 10.33 am an order to withdraw back to the third line was received as '3rd Division were to repeat the attack', a move completed at 11.15 am.

According to the War Diary the order was received at 2.27 pm that 1/Camerons and 1/Black Watch were to attack at 4.00pm. At 2.45 pm the battalion started the journey back to the front line once again, filing up the communication trench from Ritz trench near the Cinder Track. On arriving at the front reserve trench at about 3.30 pm, the

A smashed German trench.

C.O. and Adjutant reported the trench very congested, filled with troops of 1/Loyal North Lancs, and that movement was very difficult. Advice of a possible delay in readiness for the attack was given to Brigade HQ, and to C.O. 1/Black Watch, and was answered by an order to attack 'with whatever available and as soon as possible'. Only two platoons of C Company were on station to attack on time. The War Diary records these went over the top at 3.58 pm, followed by the rest of C Company at 4.03 pm directly on arrival. Two platoons of D Company, and two of A Company followed, the rest were caught up in the melee in the communication trench.

With no ladders and few steps remaining in the breastwork, exit from the trench was largely confined to shell holes – most of which were perfectly sighted by German machine gunners. Many leading assault troops were shot down before they had reached half way and the last platoons did not cover thirty yards.

At 4.10 pm a 1 Brigade order stopped any further attack. The last battle shocked soldiers arrived back in the front trench at 4.40 pm. The battalion was ordered back to the second line and thence, at 5.00 pm, back to the Rue du Bois and then on to billets in Hinges. The War Diary only notes that out of 350 who attacked, 180 became casualties.

1/Gloucesters, having waited in the reserve trenches under sporadic shellfire since the aborted morning attack, regrouped in readiness for the afternoon assault.

D Company formed up on the right with A Company to their left, supported by C Company and B Company respectively. After a short delay the battalion advanced in line with 1/South Wales Borderers.

> *Hostile machine guns fired heavily again after the bombardment. D Company suffered heavily crossing the parapet, all officers and most of the NCOs being killed or wounded. Capt Brodigan lead his company very gallantly across heavy fire until stopped. A Company could not travel so far – situation impossible – Battalion withdrawn.*

The afternoon attack had replicated exactly the pattern of the morning attack with the same inevitably disastrous results. Ten officers and 253 NCOs and men of 1/Gloucesters were dead, missing or wounded.

Captain FJ Brodigan, Second Lieutenant FH Lawrence (3 Bn) and Lieutenant WP Hefferman (3/RIR) had been killed, Lieutenant R De Trafford (3/Kings Own) died of wounds, and Captain FC Finch, Captain GB Bosanquet, Lieutenant FK Griffiths (3/Lincolns), and Second Lieutenants JH Jevons, PH Bowles, and WH Hodges were wounded. Relieved by the Royal Berkshires the battalion withdrew to Windy Corner at about midnight.

1/South Wales Borderers, with 1/Gloucesters to their right, had waited in the second and third line trenches since the failed morning attack. At 11.30 am, the battalion was ordered into the front trenches in readiness to lead another assault at 2.40 pm – later postponed until 4.00 pm. The battalion War Diary entry summarising the afternoon action is curt and simple.

> *With A and B Companies assaulting from the front line and C and D behind, the assault a failure due to hostile rifle and machine gun fire.*

Elen officers and 224 other ranks of 1/South Wales Borderers are recorded as casualties. In addition to the two officers who died earlier in the day, Captain R Woodward (3 Bn), Captain Lord ARF de Freyne (3 Bn), Lieutenant ACF Garnett-Botfield, and Second Lieutenants Jackson and A Langlands (3 Bn), were killed in the afternoon, Lieutenant NPJ Turner (3 Bn) and Second Lieutenant CH Heal died of wounds on 10th May and Second Lieutenant WT Stanborough on 13th May. Second Lieutenant Masters was wounded.

Captain AR French, the 5th Baron De Freyne, and his brother, Lieutenant GP French, were both killed on this day and are together buried in Cabaret-Rouge Cemetery, Souchez.

The battalion remained holding the front lines until relieved by the KRRC at 7 pm, and then marched back via Le Touret to billets in Hingette.

On 6 May 1/4 Royal Welsh Fusiliers (Territorials) had moved from Harisoirs to billets in Hinges, where they stored packs and, at 6.30pm on the evening of 8 May, in battle order, moved forward into trenches behind the Rue du Bois. There, as 'mopping up battalion', they awaited orders to follow up behind the assaulting troops. Two companies were detailed to assist 23/Field Company Royal Engineers, and the remaining two companies moved into front line reserve trenches behind the mayhem and, as the 2/Welsh and 2/Munsters were cut down in front of the parapets and forward movement was arrested, there they remained, under fire throughout the morning. Regrouped for the 4.00 pm attack, they struggled via a communication trench towards the breastworks but were held by very heavy fire and, 'with due regard to the prevailing conditions', were not ordered into the new attack.

The battalion was ordered back to Harisoirs just twenty-four hours after leaving. Lieutenant-Colonel FC France-Hayhurst was killed, as were Lieutenant B Croom-Johnson, Second Lieutenant JFC Hazledene and Lieutenant M Penn RAMC; Captain J Erie-Evans died of his wounds; and Second Lieutenant R Richards was wounded. 65 other ranks were killed, wounded or missing. The Commanding Officer, Lieutenant-Colonel FC France-Hayhurst, is buried in Cabaret-Rouge Cemetery, Souchez.

On all parts of the 1st Division front the earlier disastrous scenes of total carnage had been repeated. 1/South Wales Borderers, 1/Gloucesters, the adjoining 1/Camerons, and the left flank of 1/Black Watch had been ripped by fire of such intensity that before the lead platoons had advanced a hundred yards, as a fighting force, they were obliterated. The few remaining not dead or incapacitated were helplessly pinned down.

At 4.35 pm Major-General Haking, G.O.C. 1st Division, on receiving news of the checked attack, ordered another immediate ten minute bombardment on the German lines. Commanders of 1 and 3 Brigades both agreed that sending any more troops against the barely impaired defenses was a useless waste and orders to withdraw were issued.

At about 4.50 pm the German ammunition dump at Herlies exploded with a violent roar, having been struck by a 15 inch shell. A huge cloud rose into the sky and the pink tinted mist moved westwards across Aubers Ridge, causing a gas alarm to be raised in the British lines.

The German 55th Regiment, out of a total establishment of approximately 2500, lost twelve officers and 599 other ranks during the day.

At 5.00 pm General Haig issued orders that the 2nd Division was to relieve the 1st Division and effect a bayonet attack at dusk - 8.00 pm.

B. MEERUT DIVISION. Afternoon attack.

The order by the Meerut Division HQ to replace the shattered Dehra Dun Brigade by the Bareilly Brigade for the afternoon offensive was completed just before 4 pm, but nearly 200 men were lost during the move forward even before the attack was mounted.

To the left of the 1st (Guards) Brigade's positions were the lead battalions of the Bareilly Brigade. On the brigade right 2/Black Watch, in the centre 58th Vaughan's Rifles reinforced with a company from 1/4 Black Watch to replace the three officers and forty five other ranks lost to enemy shell fire during the move up, and, on their left, 41st Dogras. The other three companies of 1/4 Black Watch would follow in support.

Brigadier-General WM Southey, commanding the Bareilly Brigade, had noted his grave doubts as to the wisdom of this further attack against the same defences which had repulsed the morning attempts of the Dehra Dun Brigade, but had been very forcefully overruled and ordered to 'press the attack into the night if necessary'.

2/Black Watch, under the command of Lieutenant-Colonel WJ St J Harvey, from billets at Les Lobes, had supplied 500 men daily for working parties, digging trenches and developing the Lansdowne Post assembly areas until, on 8 May, they moved forward, first to the canal area near Vielle Chapelle then, on the morning of 9 May, into the specially prepared reserve trenches behind the Rue du Bois, where the battalion waited, battle ready, in reserve whilst the Dehra Dun Brigade attacked. At noon the order was received to move forward into the assault trenches to replace the Dehra Dun troops and to be ready to attack at 4 pm.

At 3.55 pm, as the guns lifted, the lead platoons of No. 2 Company (Lieutenant AHC Sutherland) and No. 4 Company (Captain GCS Macleod) debouched and lay in front of the parapets ready to charge. As they crept forward, timed at 3.59 pm, the lead platoons of No. 1 Company (Captain AV Holt) followed, with No. 3 Company (Captain D Campbell) ready in support. The appearance of fresh troops standing to advance after the bombardment immediately sparked the same hail of machine gun and rifle bullets as had cut the morning attempts. A wide and deep mud filled ditch ran in front of the parapets – some ten yards distant on the right and about thirty yards away on the left – the bridges laid across for the morning assault were now shattered and unusable, and forward movement was blocked. As the first waves fell the CO ordered the remainder of No. 1 Company and No. 3 Company to stay in the trenches. Half the battalion had gone over the top and two thirds of those had been struck down before they had even reached the

Sikh soldiers poised to 'go over the top'.

ditch. The barrage had again been totally ineffective. Out of the original battalion strength of twenty one officers and 850 riflemen, casualties totalled 269. Three officers, Lieutenant Hon. HA Stewart, Second Lieutenants WL Brownlow and R Sinclair and 69 other ranks were dead, and Captain GCS MacLeod, Lieutenant AHB Sutherland, and Second Lieutenants GRM Reid and GG Moore, plus 157 other ranks were wounded. 36 other ranks were posted as missing. Stretcher parties struggled to retrieve the wounded, whilst those able made their way back after nightfall. During the night the battalion was relieved by 3/London Regiment and withdrew to trenches at Lansdowne Post.

On Friday 7 May, 3ft x 3ft Meerut divisional flags, black and red quarters with a white cross mounted on ten foot poles, had been issued to each section of 58th Vaughan's Rifles, commanded by Lieutenant-Colonel CED Davidson-Houston, ready to mark the positions of their advance in the forthcoming engagement. Sandbags, emergency rations and 200 rounds of small arms ammunition per man were issued, blankets and heavy kit were stored, and briefings completed.

At 10 pm, 8 May the battalion paraded at La Couture church and then marched off via Croix Barbée, where the machine guns were off-

SOUTHERN SECTOR TRENCH MAP

134

The trench lines are as in 1916, the British front line occupying the old German front line. The communication trenches are as used to access the forward positions for the May 1915 battles.

loaded from the pack mules, to assembly trenches south of the Rue du Bois. One man in four carried picks and shovels, and company grenade parties carried forward the allotted grenades in boxes. By 2.30 am the battalion was assembled in Gridiron Trench, behind 2/Black Watch.

Being advised at about 8.30 am that, as the Dehra Dun Brigade attacks had failed, support was required, Nos. III Company and IV Company were ordered to move, via the communications trench, up to Crescent Trench. Shells were raining about the Rue du Bois assembly areas about this time and the communication trench, barely two feet in depth and much mauled by artillery, afforded scant protection. Two Indian officers were killed and Lieutenant Macmillan was mortally wounded during the move.

At noon the battalion was ordered forward to occupy the front trench ready for the 4.00 pm attack, replacing the 4/Seaforths. The 2/Black Watch were positioned to their right in Orchard Trench and 41st Dogras to their left. No. I Company on the left and No. IV Company, would lead the assault, clearing the parapets ten minutes before the guns lifted to get as far forward as possible under the shield of the bombardment.

A Company 4/Black Watch, two platoons behind No I Company and two platoons behind No IV Company, formed the second line, with Nos. II and III Companies 58th Rifles ready in Crescent Trench to follow up. Going over the top by the exit ladders at 3.50 pm the lead troops were immediately subjected to incessant fire, so ineffective had been the bombardment that enemy riflemen and machine gunners were sitting up and firing from their parapets. Those not hit crawled some forty yards to the line of a ditch where they were pinned down by the intense enemy fire and mauled by their own field guns shelling short.

The front line trench became chaotic and very crowded as the remaining two companies of 4/Black Watch moved in as the lead troops went over, to be augmented immediately by II and III Companies 58th Rifles. All became the target of heavy shelling from German Field Batteries. A direct hit destroyed one machine gun, killing two gunners and seriously wounding four others. With advance impossible, the order to withdraw when able was passed forward. Many who attempted to get back over the parapets were hit, some were dragged through muddy holes dug under the parapet, and many others lay low until darkness fell. Stretcher-bearers worked frantically after dark bringing in the wounded.

38 other ranks were dead, and 204 wounded and missing. Subedar Bostan Khan and Jemadar Sal Khan had been killed, and Jemadars

Abdul Rahman, Havindah, Harchand Singh, Kehr Singh and Hira Singh wounded. Major AG Thomson and Captain GS Bull were wounded, as was Lieutenant SA Macmillan, who died of wounds during the following night. When 2/Leicesters took over the front trenches at 11.30 pm the regiment moved back to dugouts in Forrester Lane.

1/4 Black Watch, commanded by Lieutenant-Colonel H Walker, from billets in Les Lobes, moved to Lansdowne Post breastworks on Rue des Berceaux on 8 May, and around midday on the 9th moved up into Crescent and Blackader Trenches as the Dehra Dun Brigade was relieved. A Company joined 58th Rifles for the second attack, B Company occupied the front reserve trench with C and D Companies supporting. The attack ahead halted, and positions were held until, relieved by 2/Leicesters at 9 pm, the battalion returned to Lansdowne Post.

Brigadier-General Southey stated in his official dispatch on the action of the Bareilly Brigade;

> *All three battalions pushed in part of their remaining companies following on the leading ones, but these men were knocked over directly they crossed their parapet. Each commander came to the same conclusion, that since our artillery bombardment was so inadequate and the enemy's artillery, Maxim [machine gun], and rifle fire was in no way reduced, it was useless and a waste of life to throw in the few remaining men left in their hands, and, therefore did not send their last reserve forward. This decision of theirs had my complete approval, and I decided not to send in the three companies of the 1/4 Black Watch which formed my brigade reserve.*

41st Dogras on 8 May moved forward from divisional reserve billets in Vielle Chapelle to Lansdowne Post, thence to positions near Port Arthur ready to attack and secure the main La Bassée to Estaires road. Heavy artillery fire on the reserve and communication trenches is recorded as they moved via Blackader Trench and Pioneer Trench to the south of the Rue du Bois. Progress was impeded by the many dead and wounded and so much debris and congestion that they were unable to reach the forward positions to take over from 1/Seaforths until after 3 pm. No 1 Company and No 2 Company (Captain Nixon) lead the attack from the front fire trench, with No 3 Company (Captain Dunlop) and No 4 Company (Major Milne) following in line behind, ready to occupy the fire trenches as the lead platoons attacked.

Major Milne (82nd Punjabis) was severely wounded by fragments from an exploding shell whilst bringing up No 4 Company from Pioneer Trench and Lieutenant FH Mardall assumed command.

Lieutenant-Colonel CAR Hutchinson, the battalion second in command, leading the assault with No 1 Company, received severe bullet wounds in both legs, and Lieutenant Vaughan's right arm was shattered when a shell exploded as the company dropped over the parapets to crawl forward under the barrage. The Commanding Officer, Lieutenant-Colonel CW Tribe, was struck in the chest by shell fragments as he watched his troops progress, and Captain CAM Dunlop (37th Dogras) assumed temporary command of the battalion.

In spite of continuing enemy fire throughout the bombardment and a counter barrage of HE and shrapnel on their positions, many of the leading troops had advanced to within seventy yards of the enemy breastworks before short falling shells from their own artillery forced them to take cover.

Subadar Jai Singh (37th Dogras), the sole remaining unwounded officer, sent back word shortly after 4 pm that the forward troops were ready to press the assault and awaited signal.

Meanwhile, however, lead troops of No I Company of the 58th Rifles to the immediate right were being pushed back by concentrated fire, and beyond them 2/Black Watch were trapped behind the ditch just thirty metres in front of their parapet. The lead companies of 41st Dogras had suffered heavy casualties from the intense fire and very heavy losses from shellfire had dramatically reduced the strength of the two following up companies remaining in the front trenches. It was obvious that the attack could not be successfully sustained and Subadar Singh, who by then had been hit twice, was ordered to abandon the assault, take cover and return with his troops as able after nightfall. By 5 pm only Captain CAM Dunlop, Captain RM Brind (37th Dogras) the Machine Gun Officer, the adjutant Lieutenant ELE Lindop, Lieutenant Nelson, the Medical Officer, Captain RGG Croly and Lieutenant PH Myles (QM) remained active. Artillery and small arms fire died down after 5 pm although, from the Indian army parapets, steady rifle and machine gun fire was maintained to protect those lying out in No Man's Land and to discourage any counter offensive. The trenches were cleared of debris and repaired as well as possible, dead were removed and wounded evacuated and arms and ammunition from casualties collected and stacked. About 8.30 pm the battalion was relieved by 3/Gurkhas and returned to Lansdowne Post.

Five British officers and seven Indian officers were casualties. The wounded are named as Lieutenant-Colonel CW Tribe, Lieutenant-Colonel CAR Hutchinson, Major J Milne, Captain CHF Nixon (91st Punjabis) and Lieutenant Vaughan (Indian Army Reserve). Subadar

Stretcher bearers bring the men evacuated from the front.

Gulaba had been killed by shellfire, Subadars Hamal Chand, Suba Singh (37th Dogras), Jai Singh and Lachman, and Jemadars Sawan (38th Dogras) and Dulo had been wounded. 35 other ranks were killed and missing believed killed, and 354 wounded. Out of the 633 answering roll call before the battle only 244 remained unscathed.

On the right of the Indian Corps the advance companies of 2/Black Watch and the right hand company of the 58th Rifles next to them had been shot down before even reaching the ditch some thirty yards in front of their breastworks, and the advance of the other companies of the 58th Rifles, 1/4 Black Watch and 41st Dogras collapsed in bloody heaps before they had covered a hundred yards.

Within minutes of the hopeless pitting of the infantrymen head-on against the increased concentration of pitiless machine gun fire, 2/Black Watch had lost 265 men, 58th Vaughan Rifles 258, 1/4 Black Watch 173 and 41st Dogras 400 out of 650.

At 4.40 pm Brigadier-General Southey reported that, as the German firepower remained unchecked, no gain could be made by sending any more of his Brigade into action. The shattered Bareilly Brigade was withdrawn and Brigadier-General Blackader's Garhwal Brigade was ordered forward to replace them to hold the front line.

In his account as a member of a relieving battalion, Captain WG Bagot-Chester MC of 2 /3 Gurkha Rifles describes the experience thus:

We had to advance about two thousand yards across open country to start with, but we were not fired on until we reached a long communication trench leading up to the front trench-line. Of course we advanced in artillery formation. Toward the last hundred yards or so German 'Woolly Bears' [shrapnel shells which burst with a cloudlike effect] *began to burst overhead, and 'Jack Johnsons' close by, but I had only one man hit at this point. We then got into a long communication trench leading up from Lansdown Post to the Gridiron Trenches. Here we were blocked for a long time, shelling increasing every moment, wounded trying to get by us. After a time we got into the Gridiron, where it was absolute hell. Hun shells, large and small, bursting everywhere, blowing the parapet here and there, and knocking tree branches off. Here there was terrible confusion. No one knew the way to anywhere. There was such a maze of trenches and such a crowd of people, many wounded, all wanting to go in different directions, one regiment going back, ours trying to go forward, wounded and stretcher bearers going back, etc. I presently went on to a trench called Pioneer Trench. There I had twenty-six casualties from shells. Havildar Manbir had his leg blown off, and was in such agony that he asked to be shot. As one got further to the front trench, the place got more of a shambles, wounded and dead everywhere. Those who could creep or walk were trying to get back, others were simply lying and waiting. The ground in front was littered with Seaforth bodies and 41st Dogras. From Pioneer Trench I went on to the front trench, occupied by the 41st Dogras, who, however, had very few men left, so heavily had they suffered. One of the British officers had completely lost his nerve and was rather a pitiable sight. I tried to comfort him a bit. We had to set to work at once to try to clean up the trench. It was full of killed and wounded, equipment of all sorts, and the ground in front was strewn with dead Seaforths, who made the charge this morning at 5.40 a.m. from this trench, also 41st Dogras who made a second attempt.*

As result of his gallantry, Lance Corporal David Finlay, 2/BlackWatch, was awarded the Victoria Cross. When ten out of his twelve man bombing party had become casualties he ordered the two survivors to crawl back to safety and, disregarding his own safety, went to assist a wounded man and carried him back to shelter across open ground through heavy sweeping fire. Promoted to sergeant, he was killed in January 1916 whilst serving in Mesopotamia.

General Haig learned of the second assault failure by the 1st and Indian Divisions at about 5 pm and ordered that no further reinforcements were to support failed attacks. Any gains were to be held and the troops reorganised – the 2nd Division would replace the 1st Division – ready to launch a bayonet attack at dusk.

Chapter Five

CESSATION OF THE BATTLE

Whilst preparation for renewal of the offensive at 8 pm progressed, more and more reports from brigades and liaison officers were received detailing the amount of disorganisation and congestion in the severely damaged forward trenches. Communication trenches were blocked and continuing enemy artillery fire was preventing forward movement of fresh brigades to launch the attacks. General Haig, finally convinced that his plan for a night offensive was impractical, cancelled the orders for renewed attacks at 6 pm on 9 May.

A meeting of corps commanders and senior staff officers was convened at the Indian Corps Headquarters at Lestrem and, at 7.30 pm, the commanders met to organise the re-opening of the offensive the following day with fresh troops.

By 3 am those British and Indian troops who were capable were back in their lines, and in the early hours of 10 May First Army HQ became fully aware of the extent of the previous day's losses. Total casualties of 145 officers and 9400 men (the final tally became 458 officers and 11161 men), and a low remaining stock of ammunition had been reported.

At 3.30 am General Haig convened another conference of corps commanders and senior staff, to take place at 9 am at First Corps HQ situated at Locon, 2.5 kilometres outside Bethune.

On 9 May Lord Kitchener had ordered that 20,000 rounds of 18pdr and 2,000 rounds of 4.5 inch howitzer shells, be transferred from the base stocks in France to the Dardanelles. Stocks of 18 pdr HE and 4.5 inch lyddite being exhausted, shrapnel shells were dispatched. The total available depot stocks listed on the nearest dated return were: 18 pdr 3,014; 4.5 inch 800; 5 inch 2,138; 4.7 inch 2,810; 60pdr 1,065; and 6 inch 140.

The 4.7 inch guns on the IV Army front had proven defective to the point of uselessness and fuses on many of the 15 inch shells were ineffective and not triggering on impact.

The conference concluded that, the amount of available artillery ammunition was insufficient to sustain a repeat of a two pronged attack which could last for several days and, as a sustained and destructive bombardment was necessary to wreck the much strengthened German defences, any immediate offensive action must be delayed.

Reconsidering his next moves General Haig cancelled his order for the offensive planned for the 10th and decided that a repeat two pronged attack was impractical. With only two fresh divisions available, he would concentrate on the original idea proposed by his commander, Sir John French, to implement a single front attack south of Neuve Chapelle as soon as preparations could be completed.

On receipt of the conclusions of the meeting at Advanced GHQ at Hazebrouck, Sir John French agreed that all immediate action against Aubers Ridge should cease and that his troops should regroup without delay for another single front attempt towards Festubert.

Following a four-hour bombardment of the German breastworks by heavy howitzers, an attack would be launched on the southern front only. The 8th Division was to reorganise and defend IV Corps front, only to act if provoked by offensive enemy action. The unused 7th Division however, as eagerly proposed by Major-General H de la P Gough, their commander, was to move to the south of Neuve Chapelle at once, ready to partake in the new offensive.

Although the risks of repeat heavy losses were great, positive action was imperative if the promise to assist the French Tenth Army offensive to the south was to be honoured. The 7th Division and 2nd Division were ordered to undertake the offensive as soon as possible. During the night of 10/11 May the 7th Division marched south, with a full complement of artillery and field support, from the IV Corps area, to positions north of Festubert under the command of I Corps.

News that the French Tenth Army offensive had been very successful aggravated the frustrated and considerably embarrassed British High Command. The German defences, much improved by excellent field engineering and the efficient use of well organised labour, had enabled their front line regiments to hold off the British divisions without recourse to calling up additional forces from their Sixth Army reserve.

At 2 pm on 9 May the 58th Division at Roubaix and the 115th Division at Tournai, had been ordered to stand to arms but, by the evening, this order had been rescinded and both divisions entrained that same night to reinforce the Sixth Army front in the south. The 58th Division routed through Lille – Seclin – Henin Lietard destined for the south of Lens, and the 115th Division via Orchies to the Vimy battle zone. No reserves were deemed necessary opposite the British lines between Armentières and the La Bassée canal.

By the insistent orders of senior command, without serious consideration to the objections raised by battalion and brigade commanders in the field, the useless waste of the morning attacks had

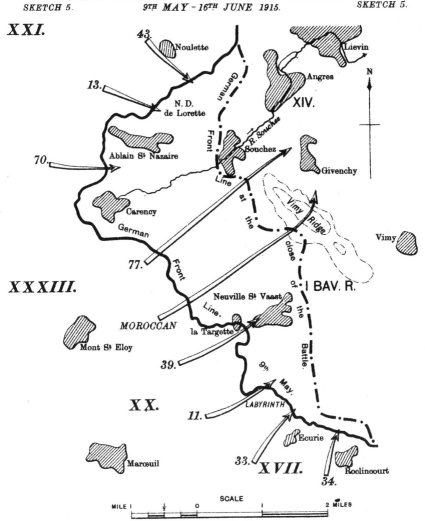

been repeated during the afternoon with flagrant dismissal of the realities of the prevailing circumstances. The British generals, acting for a country which was unprepared for war and thereby hampered by the lack of means to fulfil the demand for action by ruling politicians, had no alternative but to be seen to be doing something to fulfil their promise to the French Tenth Army command no matter how ineffective their efforts were rendered by the lack of artillery power. Considering the available intelligence reports, bigotry and inflexibility had overcome the application of good sense and countless trained soldiers – husbands, sons, and fathers – had been unnecessarily sacrificed.

Chapter Six

A SUMMARY OF THE BATTLE

Planned by the allies as an offensive over many days which would effect a major breakthrough, ultimately to reoccupy the major northern city of Lille, the fiercely contested attack at Aubers Ridge had lasted less than one day and resulted in nearly 12000 British and Indian casualties. The debacle was almost unrecorded in the newspapers of the time, attention being concentrated on the situations in Ypres and in the Dardanelles.

Followed by the officially designated Battle of Festubert (15th - 25th May), the Aubers Ridge action was called by the German official recorders, who viewed the two battles as one, 'Das Gefecht bei Fromelles' – the 'Fight at Fromelles'. The *Times*, in an article of 14 May 1915, stated:

> *British soldiers died in vain on the Aubers Ridge on Sunday because more shells were needed.*

A flippant, oversimplified, but at least partially true summary of the misjudged and wasteful attack.

The opening bombardment was ineffective and only served to warn the enemy of imminent action. The strength of the German defences and the amount of machine gun power concealed therein had been grossly underestimated. The quantity of high calibre HE shells needed to inflict effective damage to such defenses had been grossly miscalculated or ignored. The quality of much of the available ammunition was substandard, many of the guns so outdated and worn as to be ineffective and artillery batteries were rendered incapable of ranging and striking allotted targets.

Under these circumstances the advance across open ground by infantrymen was slaughter. The renewed pitting of highly trained regular foot soldiers against the immediately obvious superiority in firepower of the opposing defensive forces was totally wasteful.

Aubers Ridge remained impregnable and in German hands until eventual capture by the 47th (London) Division in October 1918.

Chapter Seven

A RESUME OF THE BATTLE OF FESTUBERT
15 to 25 May 1915

On 10 May, the day following the Aubers attack, continuing the pledge to assist the French by dissuading the German Command from redeploying any further reserves to the Vimy battle, Haig issued preliminary orders for another attack which subsequently became known as The Battle of Festubert.

The attack, from the Rue du Bois – Princes Road area, would be on two close fronts and with staggered start times. Troops of the Indian and 2nd Divisions would start the action at 11.30 pm on the dark overcast night of 15 May 1915 after a bombardment lasting thirty-six hours, advancing south eastwards from the trenches fronting the Rue du Bois. At dawn the following morning troops of the 7th Division, some six hundred yards to the south, would attack in an easterly direction from trenches fronting Princes Road. The immediate objective was to push the German line back beyond la Quinque Rue (now the D72).

The attack of the Garhwal Brigade, covering a front four hundred yards wide, had 39/Garhwali Rifles abutting the La Bassée road to their left with 2/Leicesters on their right. Alerted by the covering bursts

Making the most of a deserted cottage near Festubert, May 1915.

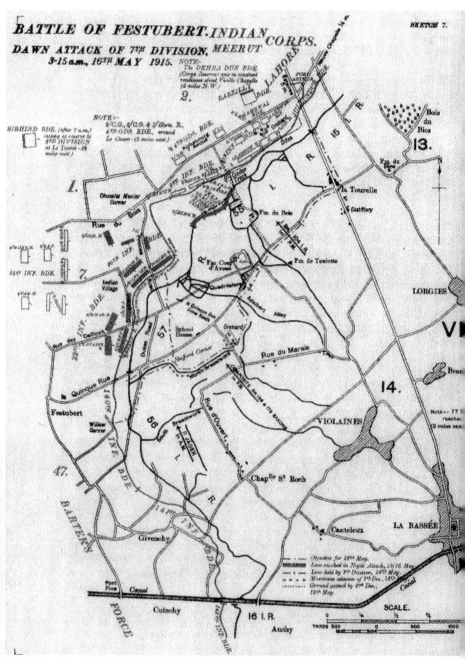

The Battle of Festubert attack, 16 May 1915.

of rifle fire from the supporting Jallundur Brigade troops, the two defending battalions of the 55th Regiment illuminated this area with flares and light ball grenades as soon as the attackers rose. The advance was rapidly halted by heavy machine gun and concentrated rifle fire peppered with HE trench mortar shells. By midnight the tattered lead battalions were withdrawn and 2/3 Gurkhas and 3/London Regt moved up to replace them. At 2.45 am after a short barrage, another attempt by the replacement battalions to advance across the ground met with the same fate. 562 casualties were registered without gain.

On the adjoining 5 Brigade front, 2/Worcesters, two companies 2/Royal Inniskilling Fusiliers and a company of the supporting 2/Ox & Bucks LI, met with a similar hail of fire from the alerted defenders. However, across the 700 yards wide front to the southwest of the cinder track, the other two companies of 2/Royal Inniskilling Fusiliers and two companies of 2/Ox & Bucks, with 1/KRRC, 1/Royal Berks, and 1/7 King's of 6 Brigade to their right, advancing silently with bayonets fixed, remained almost unchallenged, surprised the occupants, and secured and consolidated a stretch of the German front and support trenches.

At 3.15 am on Sunday 16 May troops of 20 and 22 Brigades of the 7th Division, who had waited in vain near Petillon to follow through the northern pincer movement against Aubers Ridge the previous week, rose and advanced towards la Cour l'Avoue and la Quinque Rue. 2/Border Regt and 2/Scots Guards of 20 Brigade attacked from trenches straddling Princes Road, and 2/Queens and 1/Royal Welsh Fusiliers of 22 Brigade, from either side of the Rue de Cailloux, attacked eastwards supported by 1/South Staffs followed by 2/Warwicks, against a front line defended by one battalion of 57th Royal Prussian Regiment. Although delayed by heavy defensive fire, particularly from the Quadrilateral strongpoint, the German front line was penetrated and the breaches expanded by bombing parties. CSM Barter, attached to 1/RWF, with an eight man brigade bombing party, bombed along and secured 500 yards of trench capturing three officers and 102 men. He was awarded the Victoria Cross. A trench, rapidly dug across No Man's Land by 1/6 Gordon Highlanders, was used on the morning of 16th by 1/Grenadier Guards to access and bomb along nearly 300 yards of the German front line. Although assailed by constant artillery fire the gains on the 7th Division front were consolidated, but no further progress was possible on the 2nd Division front. By nightfall, 2/Queens, 1/Royal Welsh Fusiliers and 2/Border Regt, were withdrawn, and 1/7 London Regt, with 1/South Staffs and

2/Scots Guards, replaced them to hold the newly claimed front line.

The Bareilly Brigade relieved the Garwhal Brigade in the Indian sector and the Sirhind Brigade, under 2nd Division command, took over the 5 Brigade positions, pressing attacks towards the Ferme du Biez. In action from these forward positions, as result of his extreme bravery in delivering bombs under severe circumstances to beleaguered troops, Lieutenant JG Smythe, 15/Sikhs, was awarded the Victoria Cross.

Before dawn on 17 May, a day of persistent rain from leaden low clouds, the German garrison at the Quadrilateral was shelled intensely. About 450 soldiers from the garrison managed to surrender through a killing counter barrage, before 2/Royal Scots Fusiliers and 2/Yorkshires advanced to occupy the area. Meanwhile 1/King's and 2/South Staffs, closely supported by 2/Highland Light Infantry, attempting to advance on 6 Brigade front, were denied progress by heavy machine gun fire.

Lance-Corporal J Tombs, 1/King's, was awarded the Victoria Cross having, without regard to self, rescued four wounded men under very heavy fire.

Under worsening wet conditions, with supply roads becoming increasingly congested, the forward movement of reserves became seriously impeded. The 4th (Guards) Brigade ordered forward from Le Touret could not assume battle positions around the Rue de Cailloux until after nightfall on 17th May.

Undetected by British intelligence, forward German units, supported by tough rearguard action, much artillery activity and under the cover of low cloud and swirling drizzle, were stealthily withdrawn throughout the afternoon and evening to a prepared defensive line augmented by fresh reinforcements some 1200 yards behind the original front line.

At dawn on 18 May, 2/Bedfordshires and 1/4 Cameron Highlanders

Surrendered Germans being escorted back to the 'Prisoners Cage', Festubert 1915.

of 21 Brigade, from their trenches straddling la Quinque Rue at the southern extremity of the active front, repeated an attempt of the previous evening to cross four hundred yards of open ground veined by flooded ditches, to overrun the German front line and to continue beyond to secure the Southern Breastwork on the Rue de Marais. Both attempts failed although some Camerons reached the opposing trenches before bomb shortages forced withdrawal.

The thrust of the British advance was then redirected towards Violaines and La Bassée.

3 Canadian Brigade was attached to 7th Division to replace 21 Brigade, and the 140th and 2 Canadian Brigades of 1st Canadian Division, commanded by Lieutenant-General Sir E Alderson, moved up to replace the rest of 7th Division. The 51st (Highland) Division replace the 2nd Division. The weather continued wet with mist and rain sufficiently dense as to postpone any further attack until the afternoon. Although the newly gained British positions were continually shelled, the undetected new German line remained unsighted and untouched. In the late afternoon the 4th (Guards) Brigade advanced towards Ferme Cour d'Avoue but, strafed unmercifully by machine guns and unable to progress, the attack was stopped.

From 19 to 23 May reinforcements and engineering works continued to strengthen the realigned German defenses whilst the Allied side completed divisional moves and reliefs.

During the night of 22 May, Private W Mariner, 2/KRRC, traversed No Man's Land alone to destroy a machine gun emplacement which endangered and arrested the working parties. He was awarded the Victoria Cross.

On 23 May the First Army conference decided that the Canadian and the 47th (London) Division, under the command of Major-General Barter, would press fresh attacks from the newly won and consolidated positions.

At 2.30 am on 24 May the Canadian 2nd and 140 Brigades attacked to advance their positions by about 150 yards before machine gun fire again ground forward movement to a halt. Starting at 6.30 pm, 142 Brigade of 47th Division, although suffering very heavy casualties to newly ranged heavy artillery fire from Auchy les Bassée, advanced 400 yards across a thousand yards wide front towards Chapelle St Roch and there established the new front line.

As result of a direct request from General Foch, Sir John French agreed to extend his line southwards to relieve a French division south of the La Bassée canal. The British 2nd Division was ordered south as

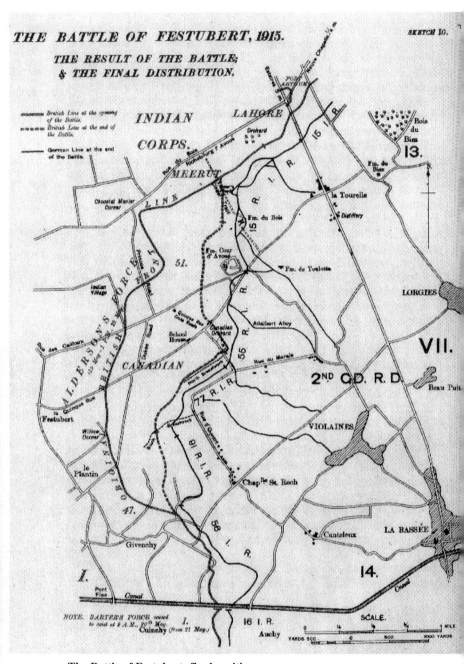

The Battle of Festubert: final positions.

150

replacement and General Haig, the strength of the renewed German line having become evident and stocks of artillery ammunition having again reached dangerously low levels, ordered a stop to any further aggressive action at Festubert. Many determined German counter attacks were repulsed and the newly established front line was successfully consolidated.

A total of nearly 17000 British, Indian, and Canadian, and 4800 German soldiers were registered as casualties in the Battle of Festubert. The Indian Army lost another 225 killed and 2300 wounded and missing, the Canadians recorded 381 dead and 1800 wounded and missing, and the British 1546 dead and 10400 wounded and missing.

The battle wrested some ground from the German defenders and was successful in drawing reinforcements away from opposing the French offensive at Vimy. Starting on 15 May, the Festubert offensive had lasted until British and Canadian action was halted on 25 May – the same day the German offensive at Ypres came to an end.

The walking wounded just out of the trenches. They wear the souvenirs of recent fighting. The variety of helmets is due to the fact that the Germans were loath to discard their ornamental equipment.

Chapter Eight

A TOUR AROUND THE AUBERS RIDGE BATTLE AREA

The best places to join this suggested route to view the battlefields of 9 May 1915, for those approaching from the direction of La Bassée or Bethune is where the D947 La Bassée – Estaires road and the D171 Neuve Chapelle – Bethune road cross at la Bombe roundabout (see pp 152) or, if approaching from the direction of Armentieres/Lille using as a start point the crossroads at Petillon where the D171 Fleurbaix – Neuve Chapelle road crosses the D175 Sailly-sur-la-Lys – Fromelles road (see pp 165).

The area is easily covered by car in one day, and the route has many convenient stopping places although, being in a rural area, please bear in mind that farm vehicles and equipment frequently use the side roads and byways.

For navigating, the IGN Carte Bleue Maps (1:25000 ~ 1cm = 250 m) are ideal, the detail is precise and all significant points are clearly indicated. Maps reference Nos. 2404E and 2405E cover the immediate subject areas of this book. Information regarding the series is available

Wistful look in a front trench. La Boutillerie 1915.

from Espace IGN, 107 rue La Boetie, Paris 75008, **www.ign.fr** or, in the UK, the maps are obtainable from Elstead Maps Ltd., Elstead, Surrey GU8 6JE (Tel 01252 703472) who provide a most helpful and efficient service.

If travelling from Ypres, by leaving the city on the N365 through the Lille Gate and continuing directly ahead you will, after a few kilometres, pass the very large Bedford House Cemetery on your left. Continue on and into the village of Wijtschaete (known as White Sheet to the Tommies of the Great War), and then to the village of Messines, where Adolf Hitler served at battalion HQ, reputed to have been located in the church crypt. Here also is the site of the 1917 battle of Messines Ridge which opened with a series of simultaneous mine explosions; one charge exploded spectacularly in 1955 to the great surprise of a nearby farmer and others still remain nearby, primed and unexploded!

Continuing on towards Armentières the road passes Hyde Park Corner, location of the Berks Corner Cemetery Extension and the impressive Ploegsteert Memorial to the Missing. Inscribed on the circular colonnade of this memorial are the names of the 11,500 men missing and without known graves from the battles of Armentières, Fromelles and Aubers Ridge, Loos, Estaires, Hazebrouck, Scherpenberg and the 1918 battle of Outersteene Ridge. With the infamous wood of the same name to the left, the village of 'Plugstreet' lies immediately ahead.

Cemeteries and places of incident and interest are scattered along the whole route. *Before Endeavours Fade,* the Rose Coombs guidebook to the battlefields of the First World War, is an invaluable aid to understanding the chronology and significance of all the various battles and the remains, cemeteries, and memorials in the area.

Continue on the N365 into Armentières and take the D933 in the direction of Lille. Turn right at the roundabout when leaving La Chapelle d`Armentières onto the D945 towards, Bois Grenier.

The interesting but busy town of Armentières can be avoided, if preferred, by turning left off the N365 at Le Bizet towards Le Touquet and accessing the Belgian N58 – this becomes D7 at the French border – towards Perenchies. After crossing the Lys Bridge turn right at the roundabout onto the D945 towards and past Houplines, and continue straight over at the La Chapelle d'Armentières roundabout, direction Bois Grenier.

As this road crosses the A25 (Dunquerque to Lille motorway) at Exit 8 – the access point for those joining the route from Calais/

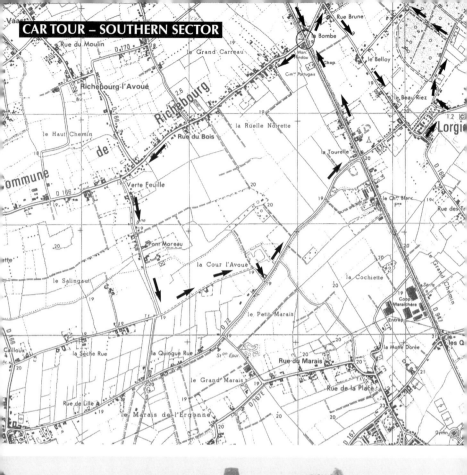

19 Brigade, Ration Farm Cemetery, in early 1915.

IWM Q5

154

L'Auberge de la Bombe, the starting place for our road tour.

Dunkirk – the road becomes the D222. Ration Farm Cemetery (illustrated) is on your right. Continue on through Bois-Grenier. After a sharp right turn the road becomes the D176. Continue and at the next T-junction turn left into Fleurbaix and onto the D171 towards Neuve Chapelle. Continue on the D171 to join the described battleground tour at Petillon crossroads.

However, for the purposes of the tour we shall assume a start point at L`Auberge de la Bombe roundabout (Port Arthur); the Petillon crossroad start commences on p.166.

From the La Bombe roundabout take the D171 in the direction of Bethune.

Through Richebourg l`Avoue this is the Rue du Bois. The British and Indian assault and front trenches, from which the southern attack was launched on 9 May 1915, ran parallel to this road about 200 yards into the fields to the left. The rows of reserve trenches and breastwork

View from Rue du Bois towards Laventie. Laventie church tower, now obscured by trees, was just visible. Rows of reserve trenches ran parallel to the Rue du Bois. Access trenches ran back to the Lansdowne Post assembly area. The St Vaast tramway terminated hereabouts.

sheltering the follow up battalions were on the right side of the Rue du Bois. Five communication trenches fed into these reserve trenches from the Rue de Berceaux and Lansdowne Post and Wood Lane trench ran parallel to the Rue du Bois to beyond Chocolat Menier Corner. Brigade and battalion headquarters were established along this road in wrecks of buildings suitably reinforced.

With the lead assault battalions of the Indian Brigade, 1/Seaforth Highlanders to the east of the La Bassée road, 4/Seaforths and 2/Gurkhas to the west, with 9/Gurkhas and 6/Jats in support, and the adjacent lead battalions of 3 and 2 Brigades, the attack was launched against the heavily fortified German defences manned by the 15th and 55th Infantry Regiments.

The boundary between the 2/Gurkhas and the adjacent 2/Welsh and 2/Royal Munster Fusiliers, with 4/Royal Welsh Fusiliers supporting, was about midway between the La Bassée road and the Cinder Track (now the Rue du Quesgniot). Beyond the track, 2/Royal Sussex lead the assault with 5/Sussex and 1/North Lancs in support and, at the right extremity, 2 Brigade front to Chocolat Menier Corner – the junction of the Rue de Pont Moreau and the Rue du Bois – 1/Northants leading with 2/KRRC and 9/King's following up.

Opposing 3 and 2 Brigades the 55th and 57th Infantry Regiments awaited determinedly with, across the whole front, twenty-two heavy Maxim machine guns, well sited, well camouflaged and well provisioned.

The 'Cinder Track', today the Rue du Quesgniot, divided 3 Brigade and 2 Brigade troops on the morning of the attack.

A couple of hundred yards walk down the Rue du Quesgniot to the end of the cart track will enable you to visualise the whole of the southern front. On reaching a sharp right hand bend in the track the small wood directly ahead now stands on the site of Ferme du Bois – a target for British 9.2" howitzers and a 1st Division objective. Looking back towards Richebourg L'Avoue from here – the German line – the whole field before you on that terrible day was a stretch of saturated, muddy, and shell pocked No Man's Land. Thousands of men struggled blindly forward into the zinging bullets and explosions to attack through smoke and debris, and hundreds upon hundreds lay injured, dismembered, or dying in agony, their vain and desperate attempts to reach impossible targets halted by resolute and well armed defenders firing frantically from their breastworks – from just about where you now stand.

The afternoon attack was a repeat of the morning scenario. Looking back from the German breastworks the attack battalions were: on the far right, 41st Dogras, then 58th Vaughan Rifles, then 2/Black Watch with 1/4 Black Watch in support, then 1/South Wales Borderers and 1/Gloucesters with 1/Loyal North Lancs in support and, to the left of the Cinder Track adjoining 1/Gloucesters, 1/Camerons and then 1/Black Watch with 1/9 King`s (Liverpool) in support. All tried but failed to reach first objectives, sustaining crippling losses in the continuous hail of fire. For his gallant conduct during the afternoon attack here Corporal David Findlay, 2/Black Watch, was awarded the Victoria Cross.

Corporal David Findlay VC.

Continue along the Rue du Bois. The first turning on the right – Rue de Charbonnier – was known as Edward Road, the road junction as Factory Corner. The St Vaast Post Military cemetery,

Rue du Bois today. It is difficult to imagine the shell ruined street. Men of the 2/Sussex crossed to the front trenches about here.

St Vaast Post was a strong point established at the head of the tramway of the same name running to the front at Rue du Bois. A dressing station was established for the Battle of Festubert, May 1915, and used by fighting units thereafter. The cemetery started in an adjacent orchard.

Rue du Bois. A statue of Christ (1922), opposite Rue de Charbonnier (Edward Road).

developed on the site of a Field Dressing Station at the terminus of the St Vaast tramway, which ran down to the assembly trenches behind the Rue de Bois, is off this road. The artillery batteries providing the bombardment were sited along Rue des Berceaux (now named Rue des Haies) which crosses Rue de Charbonnier about 800 metres in from Factory Corner. The D166 leading to Richebourg-St-Vaast, the site of the heavy batteries, is the next turning on the right – the junction called Teetotal Corner.

On the 1915 military map this was identified as the start of the Rue des Berceaux and turned right at Windy Corner into what is now the D170 (Rue des Haies).

Just a little further along the Rue du Bois, turn left at Chocolat Menier Corner into Rue du Pont Moreau – (known on 1915 maps as Princes Road).

The Battle of Festubert, which is briefly summarised in chapter seven, was also launched from the same Rue du Bois trenches by the Indian Corps and 2nd Division troops, and eastwards from Princes road and the Rue de Cailloux trenches, initially by 7th Division. The 51st (Highland) Division replaced the 2nd Division, and 1st Canadian Division and 47th (London) Division replaced 7th Division, to push forward over the latter days of this battle.

Should you wish to visit the Le Touret Memorial continue on the D171 towards Bethune beyond the next left (the junction at l'Epinette of the D166 to Festubert).

Festubert was completely destroyed during the heavy fighting to resist the German advance of 1918. A British bunker which still stands in the village, originally a ration point and officers' quarters at a light railway terminus, was home to a Frenchwoman from 1919 until her death in 1972.

On the left are Le Touret Military Cemetery and the Memorial to

Chocolate Menier Corner – July 1915.

the Missing. The Memorial, an open rectangular court and gallery, records, on panels set into the walls, the names of over 13000 British soldiers who died before the end of September 1915 and have no known grave, including nearly 1800 killed on 9 May.

The cemeteries of Vieille-Chapelle New Military and Zelobes Indian, started at the site of an Indian Dressing station, are reached by continuing further on the D171 and turning right at Le Touret village onto the D169 and then by way of the D170 through La Couture to Vieille Chapelle. An impressive memorial in front of La Couture church is dedicated to the Portuguese engaged in the battle here of 9 April 1918, and in the communal cemetery in Vieille-Chapelle is a memorial to the famous 1st King Edward`s Horse.

The British Front lines turned from the Rue du Bois and ran to the left of Princes Road until they turned again to cross this road a couple of hundred yards before the junction with Rue des Caillioux (where the road now turns sharply to the right). The German lines were just before the turning, about a 150 yards beyond the British lines. The area to the right of Princes Road was known as Indian Village – part of the Lahore

159

Rue du Pont Moreau (Princes Road) from Chocolat Menier Corner. The British trenches and the line of attack of 1/Northamptons ran parallel to the left of this road.

Division were encamped there after arrival and during the fighting at and around Neuve Chapelle in late October 1914.

Turning left at the bend will take you along a metalled farm road to la Cour l`Avoue, the site of the Ferme Cour d`Avoue, a target for the 9.2 inch howitzers, and then to la Quinque Rue (D72). Turn left onto the D72 and continue to the crossroads. This is La Tourelle which, together with The Distillery – a few hundred yards to the right in the direction of La Bassée was another target for 9.2 inch howitzers and 18 pdrs and an objective of the Dehra Dun Brigade.

Turn left at La Tourelle and drive back towards la Bombe. The German front lines and breastworks crossed this road about 150 yards before the Portuguese Cemetery – the ornate and sublime entrance is illustrated. The front lines from which the Indian brigades attacked ran through where now the cemetery stands. The Portuguese Division was engaged in the fighting in this sector from 1917 and in Neuve Chapelle during the Lys battles of 1918.

The Indian Memorial, just before the roundabout, designed by Sir Herbert Baker, is perfectly sited to commemorate nearly 5000 soldiers from the Indian sub continent, whose names are engraved upon the walls, who fought and died on the Western Front from their first European engagement at Neuve Chapelle in October 1914 onwards. A plaque within the

Portuguese cemetery on the site of the British Front Line.

The Indian Memorial.

**By the Indian memorial –
in memory of 2/Lieutenant
C A W Crichton**

memorial names additionally those who died as prisoners of war in Germany. Outside the boundary wall stands a private memorial to Second Lieutenant Cyril Crichton, 3/London Regiment, Royal Fusiliers, who died at the crossroads here on 10 March 1915 and is buried in Le Touret cemetery.

There being a lack of refreshment opportunities along the prescribed route a lunch stop at L`Auberge de la Bombe (tel: 321 27 68 95), situated at the roundabout, might be worth consideration.

Turn right at the roundabout towards Neuve Chapelle. To the right were the trenches from which 1/Seaforths attacked towards Lorgies on the morning of 9 May. The area to the left of the road was known as Port Arthur Keep. After about 200 meters take the first right towards Lorgies.

The British lines crossed this road just before the Riviere des Layes, the German lines about 150 meters before the left turning towards Aubers (Rue les Brulots). As well as the opening bombardment by 4.5 inch and 6 inch howitzers and 18 pdrs on the German front lines, a network of trenches which ran along the sides and to the right of this road were subjected to intense 18 pdr fire, and on specific strong points, heavy howitzer fire.

Continue into the village and bear to the left at the road junction in Lorgies along the D72 in the direction of Ligny le Petit (another target for the 18 pdrs). The fortified Ferme du Biez, an objective of the Indian Division, which was situated within the arc of the left turn in Lorgies, was a specific target for 15 inch howitzers.

Take the very sharp left turn after about 400 meters. This narrow but well maintained road will take you through the edge of the village and on around the eastern side of the Bois du Biez.

The southern edge of this wood, directly ahead as the road turns right along the eastern edge, was to be captured and held by the special Garhwal Brigade force (39/Garhwalis and 2/8 Gurkhas) to secure the left flank of the southern attack. They were to then work along the line of this road, secure the eastern edge, and capture the strong point off the north east corner known as la Russie. Trench lines and shell craters remain evident within the wood and several remarkably intact German bunkers stand along the eastern edge. Please park with care, this narrow road is used regularly by local traffic and by farm machinery.

The main body of the southern attack was to swing round behind Lorgies and Ligny le Petit to link up with the northern attack force at la Cliqueterie Ferme, about two kilometers due east of la Russie. Seven battalions and guns of the German forces within the wood and entrenched to the north and northeast would be thus encircled.

Continue along the Chemin de Bois du Biez through the wood to the junction with the D168 at les Brulots, turn right and stay straight on this road which, at the junction left to Neuve Chapelle, becomes the D41a. (To the left at this junction, where the road crosses the Riviere des Laies, stood the indomitable German Layes Brook strongpoint. Fire from fifteen machine guns situated thereabouts wreaked havoc on the attacking British during the March 1915 Battle of Neuve Chapelle.)

Cart track along the North East side of the Bois du Biez. The strongpoint of La Russie was situated beyond the end of the wood.

German bunkers in the Bois du Biez – used as housing by local people returning after the hostilities.

This road was the Rue de Leval which, in 1915, was continuously navigable to join the Fromelles – Sailly road opposite where now stands the Australian Memorial Park – the line of the German trenches attacked by Lieutenant-General Rawlinson's 24 Brigade, about 5 kilometers north-east from here. Continue on the D41a through Pietre and at the D41 junction roundabout turn left. The road (Rue d'Enfer) bears right after a short distance and becomes the D173, with the Riviere des Laies on the right hand side, before turning left (Rue du Tivelet) with buildings to the left. The German front lines crossed here – the opposing British lines, manned here at this point by 5/West Yorks, crossed about 100 metres before the crossroads at Fauquissart.

> Should you wish to visit the Fauquissart Military Cemetery turn left at the crossroads – the cemetery is on the right of the D171.

To continue the tour route, turn right onto the D171 (Rue de Tilleloy) at the crossroads towards Fleurbaix. The Laventie German Cemetery is situated a few hundred yards down the Rue Masselot to the left. Continue on through Picatin to Petillon.

The Laventie German Cemetery, off Rue Masselot.

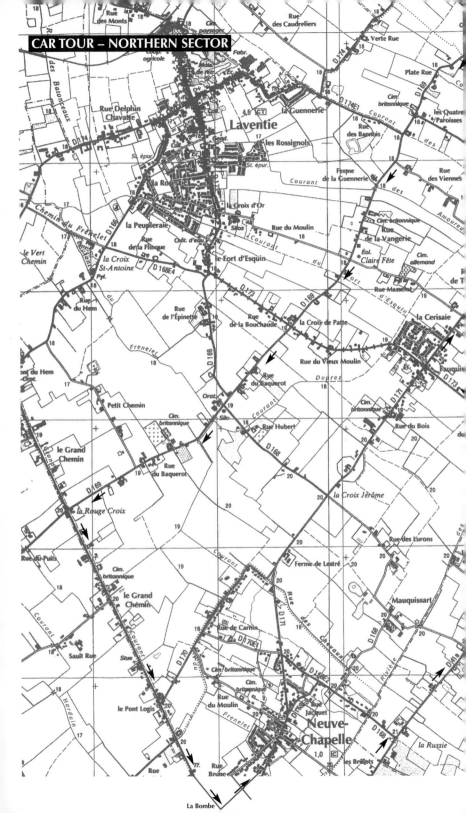

CAR TOUR – NORTHERN SECTOR

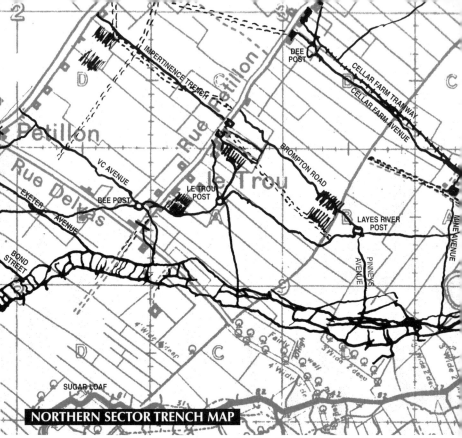

NORTHERN SECTOR TRENCH MAP

Although some names were assigned after May 1915, the approach trenches were much as used by the troops moving forward for 9 May 1915.

Petillon crossroads is the suggested starting point for those travelling south from the direction of La Chapelle d'Armentières.

From Fauquissart turn right, or from Armentières turn left, into Rue Delvas (D175) – follow the sign-posted directions towards VC Corner Cemetery and the Australian Memorial.

Le Trou Aid Post Cemetery.

Take the first left into the Rue de Petillon and park at the la Trou Aid Post Cemetery. First established in 1915, on the site of an Aid Post and Dressing Station, this cemetery, with its very attractive stone built entrance, was designed by Sir Herbert Baker. Many of those buried here died in the Aubers Ridge battle, including Brigadier-General Arthur WG Lowry–Cole CB DSO, Royal Welsh Fusiliers, who was killed in action, aged 54, whilst commanding 25 Brigade.

A substantial British bunker has settled into the field behind the burial ground. Now completely covered under the tilled surface, the only visible evidence that it exists is a large lump of reinforced concrete moved by the farmer to the verge of the field beyond the western corner of the cemetery.

Return to the road junction and pause. The cart track opposite Rue Petillon (a substantial orchard stood to its left) continued directly into the field and met the British front trenches some 300 metres in. From this point the trench line turned to run diagonally and cross the Rue Delvas just before where the VC Corner Cemetery now stands. From these trenches the 2/Northamptonshires, on the right flank of the northern force, attacked towards the breastworks of a small German salient, known as Sugar Loaf, some 300 metres away in the direction of Aubers church (visible on the skyline). 2/Middlesex and 4/Cameron Highlanders were holding the line from here southwards as far as Fauquissart. The 5/, 7/, 8/ and 6/West Yorks held the line beyond Fauquissart as far as Neuve Chapelle.

Continue along the Rue Delvas (D22c) towards the VC Corner Cemetery. To the left of the road two companies of 1/Worcesters waited with, stretched out beyond the Layes Brook in the reserve trenches, 1/Sherwood Foresters, 2/Royal Berkshires and 2/Lincolns beyond, all waiting to move up as the lead battalions vacated the front trenches.

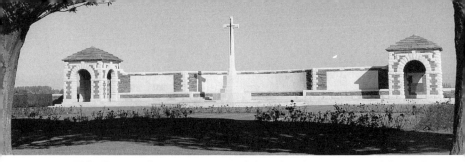

VC Corner Cemetery a peaceful and poignant memorial to the Australians killed in the Battle of Fromelles.

Beyond the Layes Brook, straddling this road, 2/East Lancs attempted their advance. 1/Sherwood Foresters would soon follow them into the same sustained hail of fire from the companies of 17th and 16th Bavarian Reserve Infantry Regiments entrenched within the breastworks opposite. Corporal J. Upton, 1/Sherwood Foresters, was awarded the Victoria Cross having, without regard to himself, repeatedly crossed No Man`s Land here under sustained fire, to treat and rescue wounded.

To the left of the 2/East Lancs, the men of 2/Rifle Brigade, and beyond them 1/Royal Irish Rifles, clambered over their parapets to attack. About 700 metres distant, the area now marked by a clump of trees, 13/London Regiment (The Kensingtons) awaited the detonation of the twin mines, laid under 21st Bavarian Reserve positions, before launching their attack.

Australian Memorial Park – Fromelles. The trench from which the attack was launched in July 1916 was the same as May 1915.

Park at the VC Corner Cemetery. Here are buried the remains of more than 400 unidentified Australian soldiers killed during attack against Fromelles on 19th and 20th July 1916. Headstones do not mark individual graves, the names are inscribed onto the high stone wall backing the cemetery.

A little further along is the Australian Memorial Park created in memory of the 1701 Australians who fought and died and the additional 3146 who suffered wounds in the attack across this stretch of ground in the Battle of Fromelles. A group of German bunkers, damaged in an

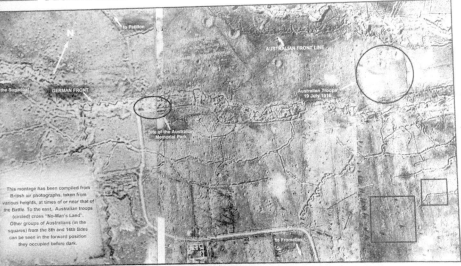

The trench lines illustrated on the plaque were the same as existed over a year earlier in May 1915.

attempt to remove them after the armistice, stands within the park, and a very fine bronze depicts Sgt Simon Frazer of the Victorian 57th Battalion carrying a wounded comrade away from No Man's Land. The Battle of Fromelles, the first engagement of Australians on the Western Front, was ordered as a diversionary action to deter transfer of German troops from this area to reinforce their army on the Somme battlefront. Troops of the Australian 5th Division and the British 61st Division to their right attacked, with the Sugar Loaf Salient at their axis, at 6 pm on 19th July.

An artillery bombardment had started at 11.00 am to be immediately answered by a German counter barrage which continued throughout the day to rain with great accuracy on the troops moving up in the communication trenches. The trenches became chaotic as wounded being moved back pushed through the forward flow of infantrymen. Troops of the Australian 8th and 14th Brigades on the left of the attack stormed the opposing trenches and pressed on, but the Australian 15th Brigade troops, attacking into fierce machine gun fire across the ground where 2/Northants had foundered in 1915, suffered very heavy losses and were unable to secure the German front trenches. The adjoining British 184 and 183 Brigades were halted by machine gun fire and uncut wire, losing over 1500 men, and withdrew

intending another attack at 9pm. Assistance of the adjoining already much mauled Australian 15th Brigade was requested and the 58th Battalion under the command of Major AJS Hutchinson was detailed to support – but the battalion attacked alone - the British attack had been cancelled without due notice to the Australians. Many more lives were wasted.

Determined German counterattacks from the open southern flank during the night isolated the forward Australian troops of the 14th and 8th Brigades who, under fire from front and rear, had to fight back through the German front trenches back to their own lines. Although agreed by the German Commander, the Allied Command refused to agree to a truce to recover wounded. The ill-planned engagement, heroically and determinedly fought by the foot soldiers, again failed to achieve success over this same battleground and the action had no influence whatsoever over the Somme battle.

A private museum, organised by the Association Souvenir de la Bataille de Fromelles (ASBF), may be viewed by arrangement through the website **WWW.asbf14-18.org** With opening times restricted it is vital that prior contact is made through the website with M. Delebarre the curator, who corresponds and speaks in excellent English.

Exhibits from the private museum organised by the Association Souvenir de la Bataille de Fromelles

The extensive Sousa blockhouses at Deleval Farm.

The mighty reinforcing 90 years on.

The German breastworks and front trenches ran along the cemetery side of the Memorial Park. Looking back across from here the whole British front is visible. 2/Northants on the extreme left with over 300 metres of No Man's Land to cross towards Aubers, 2/East Lancs diagonally across the road beyond the cemetery with somewhat less and, front and right, 2/Rifle Brigade and 1/Royal Irish Rifles with about 100 metres between them and the heavily fortified German trenches. The Kensingtons were some distance to the right.

> The next turning on the right (a distinctive red brick house stands at the corner) is the Rue de Leval (Deleval) which ran behind the German lines all the way through Pietre as far as the Bois du Biez on the left flank of the southern attack front. As a short diversion to view the mighty reinforced Sousa blockhouses near Deleval Farm, travel along this road for just over a kilometre. The huge bunkers stand to the left at a sharp right-hand bend. Deleval Farm, targeted by British 9.2 inch howitzers, stood on the right hand side about 150 metres beyond the bend. This road now meanders into the village of Aubers.

Continuing on the D22c towards Fromelles, the area of a fortified site identified as Rouge Bancs on British military maps of 1915 stood on the right hand side just after the sharp left-hand bend. Modern maps define les Rouges Bancs within the triangle between the D22c and D22 a little further on.

On the left hand side, just beyond the bend, stands a private memorial to all who fell in the Aubers Ridge attack of 9 May 1915, and

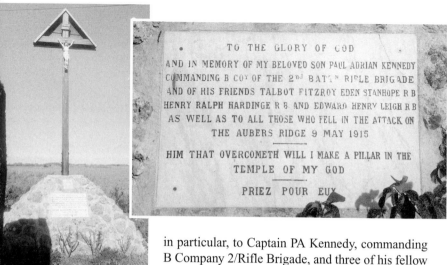

TO THE GLORY OF GOD
AND IN MEMORY OF MY BELOVED SON PAUL ADRIAN KENNEDY
COMMANDING B COY OF THE 2nd BATTn RIFLE BRIGADE
AND OF HIS FRIENDS TALBOT FITZROY EDEN STANHOPE R B
HENRY RALPH HARDINGE R B AND EDWARD HENRY LEIGH R B
AS WELL AS TO ALL THOSE WHO FELL IN THE ATTACK ON
THE AUBERS RIDGE 9 MAY 1915

HIM THAT OVERCOMETH WILL I MAKE A PILLAR IN THE
TEMPLE OF MY GOD

PRIEZ POUR EUX

To all who fell in the attack.

in particular, to Captain PA Kennedy, commanding B Company 2/Rifle Brigade, and three of his fellow officers, Lieutenants Leigh, Stanhope and Hardinge, whose names are engraved on the Memorial to the Missing at Ploegsteert.

Looking back from this point over the German reserve and front lines gives a clear view of the front stormed and held by the 2/Rifle Brigade and 1/Royal Irish Rifles with great loss of life. A section of the German support trench alongside this stretch of road was occupied and the strong point at Rouges Bancs surrounded. Access of sufficient reinforcements to secure the gains proved impossible and the attackers pulled back to occupy throughout the day a 400 yards wide section of the German front trench until dwindling ammunition and increasingly effective counter attacks forced complete withdrawal during the hours of darkness.

Continue and bear left at the triangular intersection where the D22c continues to the right into Fromelles.

> This road, which joins the D22 Fromelles – Fleurbaix road at Ver Touquet, was under 13 and 15 pdr bombardment as far as la Dreve

Fromelles Church, from Rouge Bancs a tantalisingly impossible objective. Thousands died trying to reach this.

Beside the road from La Croix-Marechal (Bois Grenier) and La Boutillerie, 2/Royal Scots Fusiliers buried their dead here in December 1915. Many subsequent burials from Aubers and Fromelles and the surrounding area increased the graves in Rue Davids cemetery to over 900.

Mouquet. The D22 road continues to the left through les Turcs, from where reinforcements were rushed to assist 10 Company Bavarian Reserve at Delangre Farm, to become D176 to la Boutillerie crossroads which were just behind the British front trenchline. The Rue Davids cemetery is on the right hand side of the road beyond la Boutillerie corner towards Fleurbaix. Taking a right turn at the D22 Ver Touquet T-junction would take you, past four more bunkers, into Fromelles.

On the right hand side of the D141 Fromelles to Aubers road stands the bunker in which Adolf Hitler reputedly sheltered during his service in this sector between 10 March and 25 September 1915. He was awarded the Iron Cross for rescuing an injured officer in the vicinity, being at the time billeted in Fournes-en-Weppes, a village some four kilometres south east of Fromelles. In 1940 he returned to pose for photographs in front of the bunker. The Aubers Ridge British cemetery stands to the left of the D41 Aubers to Herlies road and, on the opposite side of the D41, is the track leading to la Cliqueterie Farm where the northern and southern pincer movements were to link.

'Hitler's' bunker, Aubers, the scene of Adolf Hitler's Second World War photo call.

The burial ground at La Cordonnerie Farm 1915. 'Scottish Rifles Cemetery', since relocated.

Having turned left at the triangular intersection, after about 200 metres take the first left into Rue de la Cordonnerie towards la Boutillerie. This junction and the road were subjected to concentrated bombardment by 4.7 inch field guns to inhibit any movement of reserves.

About 300 metres down this road on the right hand side stood Delangre Farm, a heavily armed strong point and the objective which 1/13 London Regt (The Kensingtons) fought to secure throughout the day. They were gradually pushed back to the mine craters and the captured German front trenches, which crossed this road about 130 metres before the sharp right hand turn. The area devastated by the explosion of the twin mines under the German front and reserve trenches is to the left. The British front line, from where the Kensingtons hurried forward to take possession of the mine craters, crossed the road about 50 yards before the road turns right.

Beyond the turn on the left is la Cordonnerie farm. Cellar Farm Avenue – a major communication trench – ran from Dee Point east of Rue Petillon to the farm, alongside the Cellar Farm Tramway. Although not corroborated, Cellar Farm, where the withdrawn Kensingtons assembled, and La Cordonnerie Farm, must be one and the same.

On the site of La Cordonnerie Farm 2005. The British front trenches ran along the near side of the road.

The cart track, just before the farm, is an excellent vantage point from which to look across Major-General Davies's 8th Division attack front. The line of the British front and reserve trenches ran from here almost directly over to the VC Corner Cemetery visible in the distance. In reserve trenches immediately in front of where you stand, 2/Lincs would have waited for zero hour, beyond them 2/Royal Berkshires and then 1/Notts and Derbys (Sherwood Foresters). It was here that Corporal (later CSM) Sharpe, 2/Lincs, performed heroically to be later awarded the Victoria Cross. In the area immediately behind the farm, to the right of the cart track, 2/ and 6/Scottish Rifles (Cameronians) of 23 Brigade were dug in, in reserve.

Continue past la Cordonnerie farm and turn left into Rue du Moulin de la Boutillerie (D175). This becomes Rue des Bassieres where the small bridge crosses the Riviere des Layes. Parallel and to the right of this road ran the quaintly named Dead Dog Tramway and Dead Dog Avenue – another major communication trench.

The Scots in the front line at Willow Trench, La Boutillerie. This trench was flooded in December 1914 when a dam burst during the night.

IWM Q56198

Developed through the war by successive battalions using the adjacent 'Eaton Hall' HQ and dressing station and expanded subsequently by reburials from nineteen other cemeteries to contain over 1500 graves.

Turn first left into Rue de Petillon (D175).

The Rue de Petillon Military cemetery, on the left, was started in 1914 on the site of an Advanced Dressing Station and, as a concentration cemetery, contains reburials from no less than twenty other burial places in the area. Brompton Road Communication Trench, where 1/London Regt waited in reserve, ran from the left of the Rue Petillon, just before le Trou hamlet, to Layes Post – an important assembly point behind the front lines. Impertinence Trench connected from rear areas north of Petillon on the Rue du Bois (D171) to Rue Petillon just beyond Brompton Road Trench. A network of trenches ran through the area between le Trou hamlet and Trou Post, established about 300 metres to the left of the hamlet.

Just to the right of the road before the le Trou cemetery, 1/5 Black Watch were entrenched and, in the fields behind the cemetery, 2/Devons and 2/West Yorks of 23 Brigade awaited orders to move up. The two companies of 1/Worcesters held in reserve waited where the cemetery now stands for their order to advance.

Bee Post, another convergence of trenches, covered the area of field between the cemetery and Rue Delvas.

Turn right at the T-junction, and continue straight across on the D175 at Petillon cross-roads.

> The Rue du Bois Military cemetery is to the right on the D171 towards Fleurbaix.

Rue du Bois Military cemetery, Fleurbaix.

Beyond the cross - roads, just after the road bends right then left, in the fields on the left around Two Tree Farm, was camped the reserve 20 Brigade and, to the right, 22 Brigade, waiting to move through Fromelles to secure Aubers Ridge. They were destined instead to open the night attack across Princes Road, on the southern front, in the Battle of Festubert seven days later.

Take first left onto the D169 (Plate Rue, which becomes the Rue de la Vangerie, which becomes the Rue du Bacquerot – on 1915 military maps all designated Rue du Bacquerot). Laventie church tower, a replacement for the ruined vantage-point from which Field Marshal Sir John French and his party, including the then Winston Churchill MP, viewed the battle, is clearly visible to the right. The 13th London Graveyard, originally known as the Red House Cemetery, is on the right. On the opposite side, just beyond the road to Picantin, was the terminus of the tramway known as the Great Northern.

Laventie church spire – rebuilt on the site of the old church used as the observation post to view the battle by General Sir John French and his party.

The Royal Irish Rifles Graveyard is on the left, standing next to what was the terminus of the tramway to le Tilleloy known as the Great Central.

Between the D713 Fauquissart road and the D168 two more tramways crossed this road – the first the Midland and then the South Eastern – both started at l'Epinette, south of Laventie, and continued to the Rue du Bois (D171).

After crossing the D168, the Rue du Bacquerot No 1 Cemetery is

13th London Regt (The Kensingtons) burial ground – Rue de Bacquerot.

Rue de Bacquerot No. 1 – a cemetery in two parts – behind the farm that has remained in the Defief family through two world wars. To the right of the dividing track are Indian graves starting from November 1914.

By the side of the Port Arthur to Estaires Road, Pont du Hem Cemetery, started at the site of a field ambulance unit.

on the right hand side, behind a farm but well sign-posted. The graves of the Indian troops buried here are so positioned as to avoid the shadow of the cross being cast over them.

Where this road meets the D947 at the Croix Rouge crossroads, a bistro of the same name welcomes travellers in need of refreshment.

> To the visit the Pont du Hem cemetery turn right here towards Estaires. This cemetery was established in July 1915 by Field Ambulance and fighting units where the military tramway known as the Great Eastern,

The Rue-des-Berceaux Cemetery in Richebourg-L'Avoué started in January 1915, was increased by re-burials from Edgware Road, Albert Road, and Edward Road No's 1 and 5 cemeteries, situated in Neuve Chapelle and Richebourg.

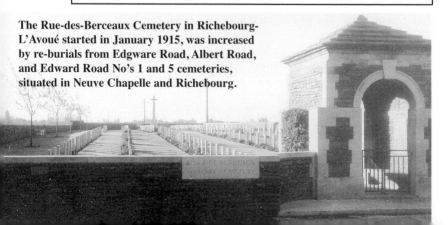

Q17322 **The ruined church and battered houses in Richebourg St Vaast, July 1915.**

which ran from Pont du Hem to the north of Neuve Chapelle, crossed the road. After the armistice remains from smaller cemeteries from the area were reburied here, and German and Portuguese bodies from this cemetery were re-interred elsewhere.

The smaller Euston Road Cemetery one of the smallest CWGC cemeteries in the world, on the opposite side of the road was established in January 1915 in an orchard behind a strongpoint known as Euston Post which stood next to a narrow gauge military railway known as the London North Western – hence Euston.

For Richebourg St Vaast, the Vieille-Chapelle New Military Cemetery and the Zelobes Indian Cemetery La Couture, Continue straight over on the D169 at the crossroads.

Turn left onto the D947 to return past Pont Logie to the start-point at L`Auberge de la Bombe. If you joined the tour at Petillon turn left here and follow the route starting from the L'Auberge roundabout. See p 152, onwards.

Q23493 **Richebourg St Vaast cemetery 1920.**

Cemeteries containing remains of, and memorials to, the dead of 9 May 1915.

Aire Communal
Aubers Ridge British, Aubers
Bailleul Communal Extension *
Bethune Town *
Boulogne Eastern *
Cabaret-Rouge British, Souchez ***
Chocques Military
Etretat Churchyard
Ferme Buterne Military, Houplines
Guards, Windy Corner, Cuinchy ***
Houplines Communal Extension
Laventie Military, La Gorgue,
Le Touret Military Richebourg L'Avoue
Le Trou Aid Post, Fleurbaix ***
Longuenesse (St Omer) Souvenir
Meerut Military, St. Martin-les-Boulogne
Neuve Chapelle (Zehrensdorf Indian Cemetery) Memorial
Neuve Chapelle Indian Memorial ****
Ration Farm Military, La Chapelle d'Armentières **
Royal Irish Rifles Graveyard, Laventie
Rue des Berceaux Military, Richebourg L'Avoue *
Rue du Bois Military, Fleurbaix *
Sailly sur la Lys Canadian
St. Vaast Post Military, Richebourg L'Avoue *
Trois Arbres, Steenwerck
White City, Bois Grenier
Woburn Abbey, Cuinchy **
Y Farm Military, Bois Grenier

Arras Road, Roclincourt
Bailleul Communal
Bailleul Road East, St. Laurent-Blangy
Bois Grenier
Brown's Road Military, Festubert
Cambrin Military
Estaires Communal
Fauquissart Military, Laventie
Gorre British and Indian
Hazebrouck Communal
La Chapelle d'Armentières Communal
Le Touret Memorial ****
Le Treport Military
Les Gonards, Versailles-Yvelines
Mazargues War Marseilles
Merville Communal

Pont-du-Hem Military, La Gorgue **

Rue David Military Fleurbaix

Rue Petillon Military, Fleurbaix **
St. Sever, Rouen
Ste. Marie, Le Havre
Vieille-Chapelle New Military, La Couture
Wimereux Communal
X Farm, La Chapelle d'Armentières
Zelobes Indian, La Couture

Appendix 1.
FIRST ARMY OPERATION ORDER NO 22. 6 MAY 1915

(a) The 1st Army will advance on 8 May and operate so as to break through the enemy's line and gain the La Bassée – Lille road between La Bassée and Fournes.
Its further advance will be directed on the line Bauvin – Don.
(b) Two cavalry corps and three infantry divisions are being held in readiness, as a General Reserve under the orders of the Field Marshal Commanding-in-Chief, to exploit any success.
(a) The artillery, disposed in accordance with special instructions which have been issued, will complete such registration as may be necessary by 5 am, at which hour the preliminary bombardment will commence.

At 5.40 am the infantry assaults will be carried out simultaneously at all points. All troops

holding the line will at the same time co-operate by vigorous fire attack along their entire front.
(b) The 1st Corps, maintaining its right at Givenchy, will attack from its breastworks in the vicinity of Richebourg L'Avoue in accordance with the instructions already issued, and advance on Rue du Marais-Illies.
(c) The Indian Corps (less 1st Highland Division [51st Highland Division from 11th May 1915]) will attack from its breastworks in the vicinity of Rue du Bois in accordance with instructions already issued. It will operate so as to cover the left of the 1st Corps, and will capture the Distillery and the Ferme du Biez.

Its subsequent advance will be directed on Ligny du Grand – La Cliqueterie Farm. La Ferme du Biez – Ligny le Petit – Ligny le Grand road inclusive is assigned to the Indian Corps.
(d) The 4th Corps will operate so as to break through the enemy's line in the vicinity of Rouge Bancs, in accordance with instructions already issued, with the objective of :
i Organising a defensive flank from the vicinity of La Cordonnerie Farm to Fromelles   and
ii Turning the Aubers defences by an attack from the North-East and effecting a junction with the Indian Corps in the direction of La Cliqueterie Farm.

The 1st Highland Division (less 1 Bde RFA) will be in General Reserve at disposal of the Field Marshal Commanding-in-Chief.

The 1st and 4th Corps will each detail one infantry brigade as Army Reserve under the orders of GOC 1st Army.

Advanced 1st AHQ will be established at Merville at 3 pm on 7th May.

R. BUTLER
Brigadier – General
General Staff, 1st Army
Issued at 10 pm.

Appendix 2.
I CORPS OPERATION ORDER No. 79.   Dated 7 May 1915.

1. The First Army will advance to-morrow with the object of breaking through the enemy's line and gaining the La Bassée – Lille road between La Bassée and Fournes.

Its further advance will be directed on the line Bauvin – Don.
Two Cavalry Corps and three divisions are being held in readiness as a general reserve under the orders of the Field – Marshal Commanding – in – Chief to exploit any success.
2. The I Corps is to attack from the Rue du Bois and advance on Rue du Marais – Illies, maintaining its right at Givenchy and Cuinchy.
3. The Indian Corps is to attack on the left of the Icorps and is to capture the Distillery and the Ferme du Biez. Its subsequent advance will be directed on Ligny le Grand – La Cliqueterie Farm.

The road Ferme du Biez – Ligny le Petit – Ligny le Grand is assigned to the Indian Corps.
4. The 1st Division will attack from its breastworks in front of the Rue du Bois.

Its first objectives are :- Hostile trenches P.8 – P.10, the road junction P>15, and the road thence to La Tourelle.

Its subsequent advance will be directed on Rue du Marais – Lorgies, a defensive flank being organised from P.4 by La Quinque Rue to Rue du Marais.

Touch will be maintained with the Indian Corps throughout.
5. The infantry under G.O.C. London Division holding the defensive front north of Festubert will be prepared to relieve the infantry of the 1st Division at P.4 La Quinque Rue, and Rue du Marais, when those points have been secured, and to take advantage of any weakening of the enemy about the Rue d'Ouvert to occupy that locality.

The 2nd Division (less 4th Guards Brigade) with Motor Machine Gun Battery attached, will be in Corps reserve in the area Loisne – Le Touret – Le Hamel in readiness to continue the advance. Troops of the 1st Div must be clear of the above area by 3.30 a.m.

The 5th London Brigade will be in First Army Reserve, about Essars and Les Choquaux [1 mile S.W. of Locon] from 5 a.m.

The 1st Battn. Queen's Regt. (less two companies) will be under the direct orders of the Corps Commander north of Bethune.

The artillery will complete such registration as may be necessary by 5 a.m. at which hour the preliminary bombardment will begin in accordance with special instructions already issued as to the times and objectives.

G.O.C. London Division will arrange for wire cutting batteries and machine guns to open fire on enemy's wire opposite Festubert and Cuinchy at 4.45 a.m.

At 5.40 a.m. the infantry of the 1st Division will assault. The troops under G.O.C. London Division will at the same time open a vigorous fire attack along their entire front.

Advanced I Corps H.Q. will be established at W.30.a.7.8 [on the Locon road 1? miles from Bethune] at 4 p.m. today.

Issued at 11.30 a.m.   R.WHIGHAM, Br.-General, General Staff, I Corps.

Appendix 3.
1st DIVISION ORDER No. 81 dated 7 May 1915.

The First Army is attacking on the 8th May 1915 with the object of breaking through the enemy's line and gaining the La Bassée – Lille road between La Bassée and Fournes, and then advancing to the line Bauvin – Don. The 2nd London Division will continue to hold the trenches on our right. The Indian Corps will attack on our left with the object of gaining the Distillery and the Fme de Biez and then moving eastwards. The 2nd Division is in Corps Reserve. A Cavalry Corps and three divisions are in Army reserve all ready to follow up our success.

The Major–General intends on the 8th May to assault the enemy's line from Q.2 on the right to a point opposite the S.W. corner of the Orchard Redoubt as afar as P.4 inclusive, to gain the line p.4 – M.10 – M.25 – cross roads at N.30 – M.32 – P.38 – R.27.

The attack will be carried out by the 2nd and 3rd Infantry Brigades, with the 1st Guards Brigade in divisional reserve.

(a) The 2nd and 3rd Infantry Brigades will relieve the 1st Guards Brigade in Sub-sections D.2 and D.3 [the assault frontage of division] on the evening of the 7th May, under arrangements to be made between the Brigadiers concerned. No troops of the 2nd and 3rd Infantry Brigades are to be east of the road running from x.5.d.3.4 to x.17.c.5.8. (King's Road) [parallel to the Le Touret –Lacouture road and 1000 yards east of it] before 8 p.m. The Le Touret – Rue du Bois road will be available for this movement.

(b) The 2nd and 3rd Infantry Brigades will form up for the attack in the entrenchments near the Rue du Bois as shown in the sketch already issued to Infantry Brigade Commanders and to the C.R.E. : the 2nd Infantry Brigade on the right from Chocolat Menier Corner to the Cinder Track exclusive; the 3rd Brigade on the left from the Cinder Track to the Orchard Redoubt exclusive.

(c) Each brigade will attack with two battalions in the first line; with one battalion in the 2nd line to clear the enemy's trenches of prisoners, to secure the flank, and then to follow in support of the first line ; and with two battalions in brigade reserve. The 2nd Infantry Brigade will also send one battalion in 2nd to work down, and to clear the enemy's trenches from Chocolat Menier Corner southwards to P.8.

The 2nd Infantry Brigade will maintain communication with the London Division troops on the right.

The 3rd Infantry Brigade will keep in touch with the Meerut Division troops on the left.

(d) The first objective will be the line P.8 – P.10 – P.14 – P.15 – Q.14 – R.14 : The 2nd Infantry Brigade taking from P.8 to the road junction Q.12 both inclusive ; the 3rd Brigade taking from the road junction Q.12 exclusive to R.14 inclusive. This line will at once be entrenched, and strong points will be established, by the 2nd Infantry Brigade at P.8 and at Fme Cour d'Avoine [Cour d'Avoue] Q.10, and by the 3rd Infantry Brigade at Fme du Bois R.8.

The dividing line between brigades during the advance to the first objective will be the Cinder Track. The Cinder Track and the Fme du Bois will be included in the 3rd Brigade front.

(e) The battalions in brigade reserve, supported by any troops which can be collected later, will pass through the front line and gain the second objective, namely, the line P.4 – M.10 – Rue du Marais – M.25 – M.30 – N.30 – Lorgies – Q.31 – R.27 : the 2nd Brigade taking from P.4 to the road junction at M.25 both inclusive, and the 3rd Brigade from M.25 exclusive to R.27 inclusive.

Strong points in this line will be established by the 2nd Brigade at the Orchard and buildings between N.12 and M.9, and at M.15, at M.19, and at M25 ; by the 3rd Brigade at the cross roads at N.30, at the cross roads at P.36, and in the enclosures N.E. of Lorgies village about P.34.

(f) The dividing line between brigades during the advance to the second objective will be the road or track Q.12 – P.18 – M.20 – M.25. This road and the buildings just south of P.18 will be included in the front of the 2nd Brigade.

The Fme de Toulotte will be included in the front of the 3rd Brigade.

(g) Troops of the London Division will be prepared to relieve the troops of the 1st Division at P.4, at La Quinque Rue, and at the Rue du Marais, when these points have been secured.

The 1st Guards Brigade will be in Divisional Reserve in localities already indicated south of Richebourg St. Vaast. The Brigade will move up to the breastworks S. and E. of the Rue du Bois as soon as any part of them has been vacated by 2nd and 3rd Brigades.

The following troops will be attached to Infantry Brigades.

Throughout.	After capture of 1st Objective.	
2nd Brigade :	1 Troop Northumberland Yeomanry.	25th Brigade R.F.A.
	10 cyclists, Div Cyclist Coy.	2 Sections 4.5 Hows.
	1 Section No.7 Mountain Battery R.A.	1 Section 4 in. Mortars.
	1 Section 1? in. Mortars.	
	Lowland Fld. Co. R.E. (less 1 section).	
3rd Brigade :	1 Troop Northumberland Yeomanry.	39th Brigade R.F.A.
	10 cyclists, Div Cyclist Co.	2 Sections 4.5 Hows.
	1 Section No.7 Mountain Battery R.A.	
	1 Section 4 in. Mortars.	
	1 Section 1? in. Mortars.	
	23rd Fld. Co. R.E. (less 1 section).	
1st Brigade :	1 Troop Northumberland Yeomanry.	
	10 cyclists, Div Cyclist Coy.	
	1 Section, 26th Fld. Co. R.E.	

When the 1st Guards Brigade is given its objective, the 26th Brigade R.F.A. will be transferred to the G.O.C. 1st Brigade.

7. One section Lowland Field Company R.E. with 2 platoons infantry to be detailed by the G.O.C. 2nd Infantry Brigade, will follow immediately behind the Brigade Reserve of the 2nd Infantry Brigade to clear existing tracks, and to make new roads.

One section 23rd Field Company R.E. with 2 platoons infantry to be detailed by the G.O.C. 3rd Brigade, will follow the 3rd Brigade for a similar purpose.

8. The Divisional Mounted Troops will be at the division report centre at La Coutre.

9. The following are the arrangements for the attack :-

12 midnight All troops to be in position as detailed in para. 4 (b) and in para. 5.

183

5 a.m. Artillery complete registration, open deliberate bombardment of enemy's position, and cut his wire.

5.30 a.m. Intense bombardment of enemy's trenches. The assaulting platoons will deploy under cover of the bombardment 80 yards from the enemy's front line of breastworks.

5.40 a.m. The infantry assault. Artillery lift fire from enemy's front line of trenches to localities in rear, and form a barrage on the right flank.

1st Guards Brigade will move up to our first line of breastworks.

After the intense bombardment all guns lift their fire to localities in the vicinity of the line of the first objective. At 6.15 a.m. they will lift again from this line, and will then bombard localities in the vicinity of the line of the 2nd objective until 6.45 a.m. Arrangements have been made for more lengthy bombardments if required by the infantry situation.

10. Flags, 3 feet square, with a white vertical bar on a red ground, will be issued to infantry brigades at the rate of six for each battalion.

These flags will be used as follows :-

(a) By the battalion of the 2nd Brigade which is to clear the enemy's trenches southwards from Chocolat Menier Corner, to mark the position of the most advanced troops.

(b) By the remainder of the attacking troops to mark any of the objectives named in this order as they are captured.

In every case the flags will be screened as far as possible from the enemy.

11. Royal Engineer Depots will be established.

Advanced Depots. One in each Brigade area near the Rue du Bois.

Main Depot.   x.5.c.8.9. [Lacouture].

A moveable depot, packed on pontoon wagons, will be located at the Main Depot.

12. S.A.A. Depots will be established at s.9.a.5.7 [on the road ? mile N.W. of Richebourg

L'Avoue]. Each Depot will contain 64,000 rounds of S.A.A. in boxes, 500 hand grenades, and 200 rifle grenades.

13. 1st Line Transport will be parked in two Echelons.

1st Echelon ½ mile north of Le Touret.

For each battalion, (except for 1st Brigade S.A.A. carts which will be in Brigade Ammunition Reserve in S.7.b. [about ½ mile S.W. of Richebourg St. Vaast]).

Brigade tool wagons. Two tool carts. Two S.A.A. carts.

Two machine gun limbers. Maltese cart.

2nd Echelon at Mespleaux [1 mile W. of Le Touret].

Remainder 1st line Transport, less 1 water cart at First Aid Post.

Two wagons for each battalion.

14. No.1 Field Ambulance will be at Locon (Bearer Division) and Hinges (Tent Division) ready to move.

No. 2 Field Ambulance will open at Ecole des Jeunes Filles, Bethune, and will establish a collecting station for walking cases at Le Touret cross roads.

No. 3 Field Ambulance will remain open at Paul Bert School Bethune, and will establish a collecting station for walking cases at the junction of King George's Road and King's Road, x.5.d.3.4. [½ mile S.E. of Lacouture].

15. The Mobile Veterinary Section will establish a collecting station near the R.E. Main Depot for casualties east of the line La Couture – La Touret. Casualties west of that line will be taken to the collecting station in Locon.

One day's rations and the iron ration will be carried on the man.

Every man will carry at least one sandbag, and a muffler or respirator as a precaution against gas. Shortly before the troops advance the mufflers or respirators should be damped with the solution provided for the purpose in each of the breast works.

No copy of this order is to be carried by anyone taking part in the attack.

1st Division Report Centre (Advanced 1st Division) will be at Lacouture from 10 p.m. 7th May. 1st Division Observing Station and G.O.C.'s Battle Station will be in the Rue du Bois.

Issued at 4.45 p.m.   G. F. Boyd, Bt Lieut.-Colonel General Staff, 1st Division.

Divisional Orders had included some new tactical directives.
At 5.30 am, under cover of the bombardment, the assault battalions were to leave the forward deployment trenches and in extended order were to move forward across No Man's Land to deploy in attack formation some seventy metres in front of the enemy breastworks.

All assault troops were issued with simple respirators which, saturated in solution just before deployment, would serve as protection against gas which had been used very recently, with crippling effect, at Ypres. This, at least, was a positive improvement on the urine soaked cloths hastily improvised previously as anti gas devices.

Appendix 4.
OPERATIONAL ORDERS 13/London Regt. 7th May 1915.

The following transcript of Operational Orders issued by Lieutenant Colonel FG Lewis TD, Commanding Officer of 13 Bn (Kensington) London Regiment, typifies the precision of battle orders issued by each of the participating battalions. It illustrates the detail of the planning based on the unquestioned achievement of objectives by artillery, infantry and supporting arms.

Information & Intention.   Ref Special Map 1/10000.
(1) In conjunction with the French it is intended to pierce the German Lines.
The Indian Corps will advance towards FERME-DE-BIEZ. The 4th Corps will organise a defensive flank on the left.
The 8th Divn will advance between 883 & 375
The 24th Bde on the right, 25th Bde on the left & 23rd Bde in reserve. The 25th Bde will advance with its right on 884 – 826 exclusive towards FROMELLES, in 3 lines from its assembly trenches.
Each of the first 2 lines will advance alternately in a succession of bounds or phases.
Each phase to begin at a fixed time so as to synchronise with the Artillery bombardment preceding it.

Time	Phase	Unit	Objective.
0.40	1	right 2nd R.B	883 – 352
		left R.I.R.	828 – 827 – 826
		13th Kens	Crater No 4 mine
			881 – 878
0.50 – 1.05	2	2/R.Berks	hedge east of 15
1.5		2/Lincs	830. 832. 835.
		13th Kens	connect with 2/Lincs 834
		1/London Regt	883

1.5 – 1.20	3	2/R.Berks	814,813,771,768
		2/Lincs	Consolidate 838,837,811,834
		1/RIR	832 to support 2/Lincs & 13th Kens
		1/London Regt	La Biette & 827.
1.20 – 1.40	4	2/R.Berks	BLONDOL FARM
		2/R B	FROMELLES

Battalions obtaining their objectives will adapt the German Trenches for defence.

Blocking parties of left Bns will work S.E.

Blocking parties will carry red flags and technical stores which will be issued near Cellar Farm under the supervision of Lieutenant Stern.

METHOD OF ADVANCE.

The Battalion will first be placed in existing trenches in spots already indicated to Company Commanders.

First Phase

At 0.40 the Kensington Bn will assault on a front of 100 yds in two lines.

First line	Left	D Coy.	Right	C Coy.
Second line	B Coy.		A Coy.	

And will capture crater of mine and pushing on to line 881 – 878 and trench to South of it.

At 0.50 D. Coy will push on & capture DELANGRE FARM.

C. Coy will be responsible for gaining communication with 2/Lincolnshire Regt near 834.

B. Coy will be responsible for the line from 879 to Delangre Farm exclusive.

A. Coy will not proceed beyond 1st German Trench without orders & will act as Battalion Reserve.

Second Phase

0.50 – 1.5

Battalion will form a strong defensive front towards the EAST & will consolidate its position.

Blocking Parties

Bombers will be divided into 7 parties.

Each party will take with it one section to make blocking party. Blocking parties will be formed up as follows :-

4 on left flank of Battalion & 3 on right.

The three on right will block till they meet the blockers of R.I.R.

The left blocking parties will work towards 873, 877, 875, & eastwards along first German Trench.

3. DRESS   F.S.M.O. less pack.

The haversack will be carried on the back. Each man will carry 2 Sandbags.

Shovels will be carried slung across the back on string. No greatcoats will be worn, but waterproof sheets will be strapped to haversack.

4. RATIONS   Reserve rations will be at the TERMINI of the two tramways in Rue Petillon.

5. S.A.A.   100 round per man will be stowed in the assembly trenches of 1st Bn London Regt.

6.Carrying Party

Each Company will detail C.Q.M.S. 4 Carriers (of whom 2 will be Coy Cooks where possible) - the Machine Gun Section 2 Carriers – 2 to be detailed by RSM for HQ. The whole to be under R.S.M.

7.COOKS   The Sergeant Cook & one other (to be detailed by Quartermaster) will stay with Bn Cookers.

8.Watercarts   One full water cart will be located at N.3 Central. The other will remain with baggage waggons.

9.Dressing Station
    The M.O. will be forward with Battalion Headquarters.

10. Aid Post   Aid Posts will be established
    N.1. b 9.4
    N.2. b 8.4
    H33 d 9.5

11. Brigade Hd Qtrs
    Lieutenant Robertson will with 2 N.C.Os (which he will select from A Coy.) report to Bgde Hqtrs at Ruined House N.9 a 3.7

12 REPORTS To Bn Hdqtrs at shaft of No 4 or west mine. Bn Hdqtrs will move forward with the Battalion.

13. Watches.   Watches will be synchronised at 10 p.m.

14. Smoking   NO Smoking before daylight south of Croix Blanche – Rue du Bois road. Absolute silence must be observed.

15. Indicating Flags.
    Bombing parties will mark their positions in the captured trenches with small red flags.
    Infantry will carry red screens with a diagonal yellow bar.
    The 7th Divn are carrying red screen with horizontal white band.

16. Machine Guns
    To be at Cross-roads H7 D. at 2.30 pm ready to march off. They will march to Croix Blanche (rendez-vous 4 pm) and will halt under arrangements of Brigade Machine Gun Officer.

17. Masks for use against asphyxiating gasses.
    Masks will be dipped in a chemical preparation under the supervision of R.M.O. Coy commanders will arrange with M.O. as to what time this is to be done.

18. Packs and Surplus Kit.
    Packs and surplus kit will be stored in Brigade Store under verbal instructions. The Quartermaster will leave his storeman in charge.

19. Very Pistols and lights will be taken up under company arrangements.

20. Transport.No vehicles will accompany units.
    First line of transport will be parked clear of the road in square H13C by 7.30 pm. The Senior transport officer (1/R Irish Rifles) will superintend this. Baggage section of train will remain in present position.

21. Maltese carts.
    Will accompany machine guns to Croix Blanche and will similarly dump their loads and return to transport lines. Sufficient men being left to carry up chats etc to Regimental Aid Posts.

22. Waggons. Company waggons will be loaded at 4 p.m. Headquarters waggon will be loaded at 6.30 p.m. Maltese cart will be loaded at Headquarters at 6.30 p.m.

(signed)   Cecil Howard Lieutenant & Adjt. 7/5/15   13 Kens. Bn: the London Rgt

187

Bibliography and Complementary Reading

National Archives Kew – Official Papers.

		I and IV Corps
		Indian Corps
		1st 7th & 8th Division
		1st Wing RFC
		Bareilly, Garhwal, and Lahore Brigades
		1st (Guards), 2, 3, 20, 22, 23, 24, and 25 Brigades
WO 95	1252 War Diary	1/1Lowland Company T/F RE
		2 Field Coy RE
		26 Field Coy RE
		23 Field Coy RE
		Northumberland Hussars Yeo Cyclist Sqn
	1263	1/Black Watch (Royal Highlanders)
	1264	1/Camerons
	1269	1/5 Royal Sussex
		2/Royal Sussex
	1270	1/Loyal North Lancs
	1271	1/Northants
	1272	2/King's Royal Rifle Corps
	1278	1/Gloucesters
	1279	2/Royal Munster Fusiliers
	1280	1/South Wales Borderers
		1/4 Royal Welsh Fusiliers
	1281	2/Welsh
	1664	2/Royal West Surreys (Queen's)
	1713	2/Middlesex
	1719	2/East Lancs
		1/5 Black Watch
	1721	1/Notts and Derbys (Sherwood Foresters)
	1722	2/Northants
	1723	1/Worcesters
	1729	2/Royal Berkshires
	1730	2/Lincolnshires
		1/Royal Irish Rifles
		1/1 London Regt
		1/13 London Regt (Kensington Bn)
	1731	2/Rifle Brigade
	1752	RFA Batts XXV 114/115/118
	1886	RFA Batts XXXIV 46/51/54
	5494	No 1 Group HAR / 4HA Brigade
	3941	1/Seaforth Highlanders
		1/4 Seaforth Highlanders
		2/2 Gurkhas
		1/9 Gurkhas

3945	39 Garhwali Rifles (1/and 2/Garhwali Rifles were amalgamated in March 1915 after very heavy losses at Neuve Chapelle.
3946	2/8 Gurkhas
3948	2/Black Watch
	1 /4 Black Watch
	41st Dogras
	58th Vaughan's Rifles

A Serious Disappointment – Adrian Bristow – Leo Cooper – 1995

A Source Book of World War I: Weapons and Uniforms – F Wilkinson – Ward Lock 1979

Before Endeavours Fade – Rose B Coombs – After the Battle Publications

Cemetery & Memorial Registers – Commonwealth War Graves Commission (& web)

Death of a Generation – Alistair Horne – MacDonald 1970

Eye Deep in Hell: Trench Warfare in World War I - John Ellis – Croome Helm 1976

I Was There – magazine series ed. Sir John Hammerton –1939

1915 Campaign in France – A Kearsley DSO OBE 1929 - reprint Naval & Military Press Ltd

1915 The Death of Innocence – Lyn MacDonald – Headline Book Publishing 1993

Officers died in the Great War 1914 – 1919 Reprint Naval & Military Press (& CD)

Official History of the War Vol II France and Belgium 1915 – The Imperial War Museum.

Old Soldiers Never Die – Frank Richards DCM MM - Phillip Austen Publishing rep. 1994

Reputations – B.H.Liddell Hart – Little Brown Boston 1928

Sepoys in the Trenches – Gordon Corrigan – Pub Spellmount 1999

Soldiers died in the Great War 1914 – 1919 Reprint Naval & Military Press (& CD)

The First World War – Holger H Herwig – Hodder Headline 1997

The First World War – AJP Taylor – Hamish Hamilton 1963

The Great War – edit HW Wilson – Amalgamated Press 1915

The Great War 1914 – 1918 – Marc Ferro – Routledge 1969

The Killing Ground: The British Army 1900-1918 – Tim Travers Allen & Unwin 1987

The Private Papers of Douglas Haig – edited Robert Blake – Eyre & Spottiswoode 1963

The Soul of the War – Philip Gibbs – Hutchinson & Co – 1933

The Vanished Army: The BEF 1914 – 1915 – Tim Carew – Kimber 1964

Western Front from the Air – Nicholas Watkis – Sutton Publishing 1999

SELECTIVE INDEX

192